One Step Forward Two Steps Back

Living with ADHD/ODD
A Mother's Perspective

Enelle Lamb

Lulu.com.
www.lulu.com

Copyright© 2008 Enelle Lamb

Published by: Lulu.com

ISBN 978-0-557-06391-8

All rights reserved. No part of this book may be reproduced in any manner, except for brief quotations in critical articles or reviews, without permission.

Editorial Supervision: Elle Fredine, RedElf Editing Services

The author neither recommends nor endorses any specific medications or treatment plans. The information in this book is of a general nature and is only offered to assist you in your search for knowledge.

Lovingly dedicated
*to my family and friends
without whose encouragement and support
this would not have been possible,*

*Most especially,
to my wonderful son,
my inspiration for this journey*

*Special thanks to my editor and friend
for the late nights and many hours of hard work*

Contents

Thunderstorms and Rainbows

Trouble in Paradise

To Sleep or Not to Sleep

The Terrible Two's, Three's, Four's...

Education 101

Mom Goes Back to School

The End of the World

Crime and Punishment

A Fox in the Henhouse

Location, Location

A Glimmer of Hope

Facing Your Personal Demons

Winds of Change

Insight

Epilogue

Sources, Suggested Reading

Resources

Chapter 1
Thunderstorms and Rainbows

Have you ever watched a chameleon? They really are quite amazing creatures, changing their colour to match their environment. Life with my son is very similar in that respect, he is always changing. One minute he is a well-adjusted normal boy, and then, out of nowhere I become the mother of the demon-child.

You know I'm kidding, well part of me is – the other part is very serious. How do you, as a parent, single or otherwise, handle the daily stress that comes with living with an ADHD/ODD child?

At times, I am exactly the same as other parents I meet – proud of my son, proud of his intelligence and abilities, proud of being his mother – but that only covers part of the time.

Any parent of an ADHD/ODD child will know exactly what I am saying.

ADHD stands for Attention-Deficit/Hyperactivity Disorder. ODD stands for Oppositional Defiant Disorder. Taken together, these disorders mean not only does the child bounce off the walls, and can't concentrate for longer than 15 minutes at a time without constant reminders; he also has an attitude the size of Mt. Everest and is not afraid to use it. Couple this with an additional diagnosis of Anxiety Disorder and some Post Traumatic Stress, and you have the mountain my son and I climb daily.

> "Attention-deficit/hyperactivity disorder or ADHD is a developmental disorder of self-control. It consists of problems with attention span, impulse control, and activity level."
>
> Russell A. Barkley, PhD
> Taking Charge of ADHD

Let me back up a bit and introduce myself.

I am the single mother of an extraordinary boy, and this is our story.

Imagine if you will, a slender, blonde, tousle-headed young man with a radiant smile and fierce hug. On the surface, he appears to be a typical youngster in every way.

He arrived in this world on May 27, 1997 several days late, at an ungodly hour of the morning, having decided that he was finally ready to make his entrance. After an interminable amount of hard work and coaxing on my part, he finally joined us. This attitude, I must confess, pervades his life to this day.

When he was returned to me after being weighed and measured, I was reassured by his quiet perfection. I didn't realize while looking into his face, that this would be the beginning of an incredible relationship, and one of the few blessed moments of quiet.

My son was diagnosed with ADHD/ODD at the age of six. While not all of this was apparent during his infancy, there were facets of his budding personality that, upon looking back, hinted that parenting him would become the most challenging role of my life.

Having already successfully parented one child, I felt I was qualified to handle the challenges of my second one. True, I was entering my 40's when I had him, but really, how hard could it be? I had, by now, weathered erratic feeding patterns, colic every night from 7 p.m. to midnight for six months, immunizations, toilet training, ear infections, and numerous other trials that are part and parcel of rearing a small person.

Even given the fact that all children are different, they still have the same basic needs...right? I couldn't have been farther from the truth.

Have you ever marvelled that parents of more than one offspring discover not one of their children is the same as its siblings? I know I asked myself that question more than once after finding out nothing I had done to parent my daughter worked for my son.

It was as if he was of a different species, not at all related to his sister.

From the day I brought him home, he cried. I tried every colic remedy known to man. I also tried vacuuming, going for walks, driving endlessly, rocking him, feeding him, and changing him. In short, I tried anything I had ever been told, and nothing worked.

I should correct that statement. Some things did work off and on, but it was hit and miss – more miss, to be honest. I felt like a first-time mother. Here I was with a wealth of experience, none of which was the least bit useful when it came to my son. He was a different story. For whatever reason, he just did not respond to the methods I had learned or read about.

> "ADHD is often associated with other behavioural and emotional disorders. From early infancy, children with ADHD are often reported to be more demanding and difficult to care for in their general temperament than are children without ADHD."
>
> Taking Charge of ADHD

It would have made my life easier, knowing then what I know now.

I'm sure I still would have struggled to find a happy medium, but at least I'd have had some guidelines.

The hardest thing for any parent to come to grips with is realizing their child is different.

Knowing there are other parents facing similar challenges is a huge relief. Finding someone who is weathering the same storm isn't always easy though, especially before your child has been diagnosed.

No one I spoke to had experienced what I was going through. Most looked at me with disbelief, saying, "Oh, it can't be that bad, have you tried..." and offered their suggestions. I didn't discount their ideas. I was desperate to see if they held the solution to my problems – only to discover they didn't.

At times, I felt as if I had become a reluctant member of an ultra-exclusive club and the secretary had neglected to give me the rules or meeting times.

Welcome to my world.

Now, I'm not saying the professionals don't know anything. The ones who specialise in ADD/ADHD/ODD are up to date on all the clinical information, and once you and your child have run the gauntlet of tests, you become privy to that information.

However, you must first cross a very large no man's land, rife with misinformation, well-intentioned but poor information, and downright bad information before you can claim your prize.

For me, the crossing took six long, hard-fought years.

Chapter 2

Trouble in Paradise

You might be asking yourself "What took me so long? Surely you had an inkling that something was not quite right?"

My first clue that my son was indeed going to be a challenge was when I asked the hospital night nurse how he had slept and was told "...restless." Let me tell you, that didn't even begin to cover his sleep patterns! After bringing my son home from the hospital, I quickly learned that his idea of sleeping through the night was nothing like mine.

I erroneously thought I could feed him, change him, and voila, he would be ready for a nap. He, on the other hand, had different ideas. I counted myself as fortunate when my bundle of joy slept for two continuous hours and heaven help me if I tried to move him. I soon discovered, by trial and error, that getting him to sleep was only half the battle. Keeping him that way proved to be just as difficult. He refused to sleep anywhere except on my chest or beside me in his car seat. I spent the first four months of my son's life trying to get him to sleep longer than two hours at a stretch, with virtually no success.

This was an exceedingly frustrating period for me, made harder because my son appeared to have no problems sleeping when he stayed at his grandma's house.

About once a month, she would take him overnight. She called it "getting her kid fix": I called it a much-needed break. I remember, after the first time he stayed overnight, I asked how he had slept, and was stunned to hear her tell me he slept through the night!

Now, I know children always act differently when their parents aren't around, but he was just a baby! ...and this was not an isolated incident. Every time my son spent the night at grandma's house (I love that phrase don't you?) he would sleep through the night.

She couldn't understand why I was saying I had so much trouble with him at bedtime, and I couldn't figure out why my little angel would sleep for her and not me! Years later, the only thing we could come up with was that she would listen to classical music at night, something that was never heard at our house, as my husband was a fan of heavy metal, hard rock and video games.

True, he didn't play his music while I was trying to put our son to bed, but, as my mother-in-law pointed out, the atmosphere was different. Secretly, I think she used to put brandy in his pabulum!

You can imagine my absolute elation when he finally slept a solid four hours! He had graduated from sleeping in his car seat to a full sized stroller by this time and could sit upright, albeit propped, during the day.

I had put him in his baby swing in front of the television, with the hopes that I could get him to nap. I was exhausted, and the swing's automated mechanism only ran for fifteen minutes, so I attached my housecoat tie to the back of the seat, thereby providing me with a very effective, functional apparatus to rock my son. I must admit to being very pleased with my ingenuity.

When my daughter came home from school, she found me lying on the couch, napping and pulling the housecoat tie. She maintains to this day that many times I would move my hand to pull the tie, *with nothing in my hand*! Somehow, I don't remember it like that at all!

Thinking I had stumbled upon the magic formula to coax my child to nap, something he rarely if ever did, I was eager to repeat the performance the next day. After a half hour of false starts, he finally drifted off to sleep. Imagine my disappointment, when only another half hour passed and he was awake – for the rest of the day! Talk about a grumpy mommy.

I found the first year of my son's life totally exhausting. I would like to say that he outgrew his insomnia, along with his need to sleep with me, but unfortunately, that was not the case. Until he was six months old, it was normal for me, after a long night in the trenches, to finally get him to sleep in time to say good morning to my daughter, who was getting up for school.

Night after night, I would sit up with my son, rocking him and pleading with him to *"Please* fall asleep."

Of course, my husband needed his sleep in order to work his part-time job, so I was the only candidate available for the task. As my daughter was only in Grade 6 at the time, I refused to consider delegating even part of the night watch to her.

I have since come to realise that being consistent plays a big role where these children are concerned – another tidbit of information I gleaned much later in the struggle.

Unfortunately, I didn't put it into practice as early or as often as I should have.

One lesson I was quickly learning in dealing with my son was the art of compromise. I can't recall how many hours I spent fighting with him, trying to get him to comply with my wishes, only to lose. This of course only added to my level of frustration. As you can tell, we did not have an idyllic mother/son relationship!

My daughter, the child of a previous marriage and eleven years older than my new son, was amazing during that first year. Without her help, I would have been a candidate for a rubber room. She would come home from school, plop her brother in his stroller and take him for a walk to give me a break. I'm sure I don't have to tell you what I did with that free time – Mommy naptime!

I felt terribly guilty asking her for help, but I wasn't getting much from my son's father. His idea of helping was to tell me I should nap when our son did.

On many occasions when I asked for help, I would hear "In a minute." Well, "in a minute" was usually far too long to wait most of the time, so my daughter stepped up to the plate. She pitched in and changed diapers, made bottles, and looked after many of the little things around the house to take some of the load off me.

She proved to be an excellent maker of pabulum and porridge. She came with me on weekly grocery-shopping walks and many of the numerous trips to the emergency room.

In fact, she and I made so many trips there in the first two years that we were almost on a first name basis with the emergency nurses.

> "...children with ADHD are more likely to experience all forms of accidental injury...the medical costs associated with raising a child with ADHD have recently been found to be more than double those for raising a normal child...with more frequent visits to the local hospital emergency room."
>
> Russell A. Barkley, PhD
> Taking Charge of ADHD

Remembering those trips, one particular story comes to mind for both of us. My son, age two at the time, had been playing outside on the patio, and I asked my daughter to bring him in for supper. He was wearing a fuzzy hoody-type jacket, and she was having trouble getting it over his head.

I recall telling her to just pull it off and put him in his highchair to eat, which she did. He had been crying because he didn't want to come in, so neither of us paid much attention when the tears didn't stop immediately.

He settled down in his chair and started eating, but I noticed he was using his left hand. This wasn't unusual as he often traded hands several times during a meal, but what was different was the fact that he *didn't* change hands.

I watched closely while he ate, and noticed there appeared to be something not quite right with his right arm, so after I helped him finish his meal I told my husband, who had been playing video games throughout, that I was taking our son to the emergency room.

My daughter and I bundled him up, and off we went. After seeing the doctor and getting the necessary x-rays done, we were told there was nothing wrong. However, he told me, it looked like the arm had been dislocated. Dislocated, how was that possible? He replied that it was quite common and very easy to do, usually by simply tugging on the arm.

My daughter and I looked at each other in horror. The jacket! She immediately burst into tears because she had done this horrible thing. I felt like the worst mother on earth, consoling my daughter, all the while thinking the doctor was going to write me up for abusing my son.

Thoroughly chastened, we left the hospital, with a now very calm, quiet boy. As soon as we got in the door, we retrieved the jacket and threw it in the garbage!

Since I opened a can labelled 'abuse', I will relate a particular occurrence that stands out in my mind.

This particular morning, I had sent my daughter off to school and followed my son to bed, only to be wakened two hours later by an extremely fussy boy. I decided right then that I knew why many species of the animal kingdom eat their young!

Picture, if you will, an incredibly frustrated, sleep-deprived, exhausted mother, doing her best to cope with running a household while seeing to the needs of a husband, a school aged daughter, and an inconsolable baby. I couldn't take anymore, and I snapped.

Thoughts of picking him up and shaking him or bouncing the stroller so hard he would fall out raced through my head. The more he screamed, the worse they grew. It was as if a dull red haze was clouding my mind.

Desperate, I looked for something other than my son on which to take out my frustration.

Mental pictures of smashing plates or putting my fist through the wall flashed through my mind, only to be vetoed by my voice of logic. After all, it told me, I would be the one cleaning up the mess! I could hear my son crying in his stroller behind me, but I was on a mission. I had to get this haze out of my head.

Frantic, I scanned the room, looking for something, anything. The cordless phone! I picked it up and smacked myself in the forehead with it. After four years of studying Tae Quon Do, it wasn't a love tap.

Surprisingly, I didn't feel a thing, so I did it again. Still nothing! I remember looking at the phone in my hand and thinking how strange it was that I hadn't felt anything.

As I write this, I can see myself standing there as clearly as if it were yesterday. I took the phone and hit myself repeatedly on the forehead, counting as I did it.

When I reached the count of four, my brain finally registered pain and I stopped. The red haze disappeared and I could see normally again. After checking to make sure the phone still worked, I put it down, rubbed my forehead, took a deep breath, and went to look after my son.

I can't say I'm proud of my actions. In fact, I feel very silly and rather embarrassed relating this to you, but I was fortunate. I have read horror stories of abuse. Many people have asked me how anyone could hurt an innocent child, and my mind flashes back to that day.

It scares me to realize how close I came to hurting my son, but thankfully, I managed to dodge that bullet.

Chapter 3

To Sleep, or Not To Sleep

I suffered months of aggravation before I stumbled onto a way to get my son to stop crying incessantly. Out of sheer frustration, I picked him up, looked him in the eye and told him if he didn't stop screaming I was going to bounce him on his pointy little head. Upending him, I bounced him up and down, allowing his head to brush my lap before hoisting him aloft for another bounce.

The screaming stopped. Can you imagine? There he was, five months old and upside down with a huge grin on his face. Amazingly, that tactic worked for months, and I must tell you it was very rare for anything to work for very long.

Around that same time, I decided to move him from his make shift bed into his crib. I had tried for months to get my son to sleep in his crib.

I would lay him down, and he would immediately start screaming. I tried to get him to sleep first, and then put him in the crib. However, most times, within minutes of his head hitting the pillow, he was awake.

I talked to my family doctor about how impossible it was to familiarize my son with his new sleeping arrangements. He told me it was not uncommon to go through a difficult transition period, and gave me instructions on how to ease him into his new bed with a minimum of fuss.

Armed with his words of wisdom, I decided to put it to the test that very night. The plan was to put my son in his crib, and leave the room. I was told to let him cry for no more than fifteen minutes, then go in, reassure him, and again leave the room, the premise being he would realise I was still there and settle down to sleep. I was to repeat this as often as necessary, and was assured my son would only cry for about an hour or so.

After five hours of screaming, several phone calls from irate neighbours, and some twenty trips to reassure my son, I gave up. I decided that, if the only way for me to get a somewhat decent night's sleep and preserve my sanity was to let my son sleep with me, then so be it.

For the next six months, I spent my nights sandwiched between my son and my husband.

There are two schools of thought about allowing your child to sleep in your bed. One says it's good for their development and strengthens the bond between parent and child. The other holds it's detrimental to the child and fosters a dependence on the parents that becomes harder to break as the child gets older. Personally, I didn't give a rat's patootie about any of that. I needed sleep!

I wasn't thrilled with the situation. There I was between two very active sleepers, trying to dodge elbows and knees, make sure my son didn't roll off the bed by accident, and hopefully grab a few minutes of shuteye. Having spent more sleepless nights than I cared to remember, I felt this was by far the better solution.

In an effort to remain positive, I thought perhaps my son's aversion to sleeping in his crib was due to a comfort factor – after all, those mattresses are not exactly built for a relaxing night's sleep.

As well, one can only be the filling of an Oreo cookie for so long. Shortly after my son's second birthday, we relocated to a three-bedroom house and he moved into his own room with a regular twin sized bed, minus the legs.

My reasoning for this was twofold. I reclaimed my side of the bed, and my son would have his own space, surrounded by his favourite things. I hoped this would create a sense of comfort and belonging for him, and he would want to stay in his own room.

My son seemed quite pleased with his very own room. He had his toys and stuffed animals all together instead of stored in different places, plus he had his own space to play. He still scattered his things throughout the house, but I at least had the option to put him in his room to play instead of having to share my living room all the time.

To my delight, he absolutely loved his new bed. He bounced on it, built forts with the blankets, converted it into a racetrack one day and an army base the next, but come bedtime refused to stay in it more than five minutes at a time. There went the comfort and belonging theory down the tubes.

I now added another job to my list: keeping my son in his bed long enough to fall sleep. Of course, my husband worked evenings, so he couldn't help, although occasionally I managed to convince him to take a turn.

As my son was an extremely active child, he would toss and turn trying to get comfortable. I discovered that the trick to getting him to fall asleep was to keep him still for five minutes. If I could get him to do that, I would have a few hours rest before he woke up again.

In order to accomplish this, I would lie beside him in the bed and throw my leg over top of him to keep him still, all the while repeating, "Lie still please, it is bed time." However, even though the system worked, it wasn't the quickest or easiest. It could take hours before I got him settled enough to sleep.

I had been told that some children, including me, when I was young, have trouble falling asleep because there is an absence of noise in their room, which heightens the sounds in the rest of the house. That made sense to me.

Have you ever spent the night in a hotel and noticed how the quiet seemed to amplify the surrounding noises? Well, one way to rectify that situation is to have a fan running in the room. The white noise helps to soften any intrusive sounds from outside the bedroom, and you are able to fall asleep.

Another method is to have a radio playing in the background. This works the same way as the fan – as long as you have it on a station that plays soothing music.

I immediately adopted both methods. Separately, they had no apparent effect on my son's sleeping habits, but when I combined the two, they seemed to work, at least part of the time.

As my son grew older, our routine changed slightly. Although I didn't have to place my leg over him to keep him from squirming, I constantly had to tell him to stop talking. Why is it that since the beginning of man, in children of all ages, the word "bedtime" triggers them to tell you about their days activities?

We finally settled into a routine – lights off, fan on, radio on, and me, stretched out beside him on the bed. Unfortunately, I would be ready to fall asleep long before my son.

I couldn't think of a single reason why my son constantly refused to go to sleep at night, aside from the natural aversion all children have for bedtime. It couldn't be due to separation anxiety – he saw me every single moment of the day.

As well, according to my mother-in-law, he had no trouble sleeping at her house. So why was it that he didn't stay in bed, even after being threatened with a spanking, or grounding?

> "Children with ADHD do not benefit from warnings about what is going to happen later. They seem to base their behaviour on what is at hand rather than on information about future events."
>
> Russell A. Barkley, PhD
> Taking Charge of ADHD

Even professionals, who study ADHD/ODD, prescribe putting the child to bed and leaving the room. When, not if, the child gets up you take him back to his room and put him back to bed. They say to repeat this as often as necessary, and the child will learn to fall asleep on his own.

Who the heck are they trying to kid? I followed that advice, doing my best to be consistent, to no avail.

The necessity of being consistent is drilled into you after diagnosis, and for good reason. As they can be very manipulative, these children need to hear unvarying, calm, and clear repetition of the desired behaviour to be able to moderate their actions.

This constant battle at bedtime was physically and mentally exhausting – the last thing I wanted or needed at the end of a very long day.

For seven years, I waged a nightly war, trying to get my son to bed and keep him there. Even though I did everything humanly possible, short of resorting to duct tape, it was normal to have him fall asleep as late as midnight or one o'clock.

It wasn't until I moved out on my own and the world as we had known it came to an abrupt end, that I discovered Melatonin, a non-prescription, herbal sleep aid. One little pill an hour before bedtime and for the first time since my son was born, he was asleep before 9 o'clock at night. Mind you, I still had to lie down with him and keep up the "Stop talking, please," litany, but it only lasted, on average, twenty minutes. That was a small price to pay for a very large return.

I have realised, since travelling down the ADHD/ODD road, that having difficulty sleeping is common with many of these children. Unfortunately, since the diagnosis cannot be made before the age of six, or so I am told, many parents fight this battle blind. For that matter, the most that doctors and paediatricians recommend are old methods that do nothing to help with a child who has irregular or nonexistent sleep patterns. Warm milk and a hot bath is, to these children, an invitation to stay up longer, not a means to fall asleep.

Several of my friends suggested valium, duct tape and a rubber mallet.

Each parent I spoke to regarding their child's not sleeping had never been told of non-prescription medication by their family doctor/paediatrician. If they learned about it at all, it was through a chance encounter with another family in a similar situation, or a desperation driven attempt to find something that would work.

The relief I experienced the first night I gave my son Melatonin is something I will never forget. I can remember wandering around the house looking at the clock thinking, "Oh, my God! I can actually watch some TV and relax!" Something, I might add, I had been unable to do since I brought him home from the hospital. I felt like I had won the lottery.

You will be forgiven for thinking that since I was now armed with a magic formula for the bedtime routine, it would be a cinch to get him to sleep. Well, the actual sleeping part usually takes anywhere from five minutes to half an hour to achieve, depending on how tired he is. I still have to make sure he gets ready, which means I have to either physically start the undressing process, or constantly prompt him. The politically incorrect phrase is "nag the hell out of him."

Believe me when I tell you I would give almost anything not to have to do that.

I used to watch my friends with envy when they put their kids to bed. It seemed that all they had to do was sweetly murmur "Time to wash up...bedtime," and presto! Their kids were washed, teeth brushed, jammies on, kisses all round and into bed. You have no idea how much I would have given to be able to do that, but with my son, nothing is ever simple.

I accept that living and dealing with this disability is a learning experience, but there has to be a better way. I spent years frustrated, exhausted, overworked, ostracized and misunderstood before my son was diagnosed.

Until that time, there seems to be only one pattern available for raising a child, and if the information offered by public health nurses, doctors, or even other mothers doesn't work, you are on your own.

The reason for the long journey to diagnosis is, in part, to avoid labelling those children as ADHD who will eventually grow out of their usually much milder symptoms or behaviours. Understanding this does not make the wait any easier.

In the meantime, though, none of these professionals to whom I took my son seemed willing to do more than note down his behaviours. It was not until he grew older, that they actually began to look for solutions to some of our challenges.

What is needed is a parenting book that gives alternate methods for parents who have used the tried and true process with no results.

Chapter 4

The Terrible Two's, Three's, Four's...

By the time he was four months, my son's ADHD, although not yet diagnosed, was noticeable. Where most children of that age are fascinated by the images on a television screen, my son showed absolutely no interest. The only thing that captured his attention was the occasional thirty-second commercial break.

As he grew older, it appeared that nothing could maintain his interest for longer than five minutes. He was constantly on the move from one thing to the next, leaving a trail of discarded objects in his wake.

Now, most people would read this and think I was jumping at shadows. How could I possibly know my son was different from other children? I will be the first to say I questioned myself many times. I would tell myself it was just a quirk of his personality. It wasn't as if he were totally introverted, but he definitely wasn't showing any interest in books, television shows, music, or any social interaction with other toddlers.

I remember reading to my nephew when I babysat, and recall watching him, as he would follow the story and pictures. My son, on the other hand, was soon squirming to get down. He reacted the same way to children's television programming. There didn't seem to be anything that would hold his interest for more than a few minutes at a time.

Until my son was three years old, I had a very busy boy on my hands. Then, completely by accident, a major breakthrough occurred.

A friend had loaned me their copy of Toy Story, a Disney movie, and while my son was held captive in his highchair eating lunch, I popped it in the VCR.

For the first time ever, he was completely engrossed. He enjoyed the video so much; he watched it nineteen times in the next week alone! To say it became a favourite would be an understatement. We watched it so many times over the ensuing month that I still know most of the dialogue, as well as the lyrics of the theme.

This was to become a pattern for the next few years. The new video reigned as the flavour of the month, to be viewed incessantly until the next flavour was discovered.

My sister immediately boxed up her kid's collection of now-unwatched Disney videos and sent them to us. From then on, whenever I needed to do housework undisturbed, I just popped in a favourite movie. I'm not ashamed to admit that I even used them as a way to snatch a short nap. I would make sure my son had juice and a snack, put him in his chair and lie down in his room until the movie over, or until he let me know he needed something.

Karma is not something you want to mess with, but when I was a kid, it was something I knew nothing about.

Stay with me on this...

My mother was raised to eat what was put in front of her, no questions asked, and she tried to raise us the same way. Not until we became teenagers, were we considered mature enough to decide what foods we preferred. I must admit I was more of a challenge than my siblings.

When my mother prepared a meal, she wouldn't tell me what she put in it, because if I knew it contained anything unfamiliar or, heaven forbid, onions or garlic, I wouldn't want to eat it. She became skilled in the art of camouflage. Still, until I reached an age where I could serve myself, and was allowed to politely refuse certain foods, I spent many evenings sitting at the dinner table, finishing my supper alone.

It was no surprise when my son began exhibiting signs of being a picky eater. This is where Karma comes in. I really had expected nothing less of any child of mine.

Until he graduated from pureed baby food, there was no problem. However, as soon as he was introduced to textured, chunky foods, all bets were off!

He refused to eat any type of fruit. As soon as he found a lump, he quit eating. Rather than buy jarred vegetables, I fed him portions of our meals, and for the most part that worked. But as soon as he became more proficient with feeding himself, the menu dwindled.

Where he used to eat pan-fried potatoes, only French fries or mashed potatoes were now acceptable – but not pork, fish, onions, mushrooms or tomatoes and no soup of any kind. He would eat an apple; but not applesauce, drink orange juice but not eat oranges; and no pears, cherries, strawberries, raspberries, blueberries…well, you get the picture. The only other fruit he would eat was and is, to this day, an occasional banana.

The list kept getting smaller and smaller, and my job kept getting harder. I was ready to tear out my hair! Not only did I have a son who bounced off the walls from 8 a.m. until after midnight most nights, now he wasn't eating. I remember thinking it can't get any worse than this. Boy, was I wrong!

Getting my son to eat had become such a challenge, my daughter or I would sit beside him at the table, and as soon we could see he was losing interest, we would take over feeding him.

As he got older, my daughter took the art of encouraging him to eat to the next level. I would inspect his plate and tell him he only had to eat two more bites. If the bite he took was too small, my daughter would say, "Oh come on, that wasn't a bite...there wasn't anything on the fork!" or, "That doesn't count, it was too small!"

By the time she was finished showing him what constituted a proper sized bite, he had generally cleaned his plate. This strategy worked extremely well when we had to attend family functions, or, heaven forbid, sit in a crowded restaurant.

Believe it or not, although my son is now several years older, we can still sometimes successfully employ her tactics.

I should point out that my daughter wasn't always a Florence Nightingale. Most of the time she was more like Dr. Jekyll and Mr. Hyde, flipping from selfless devotion to acting out in angry disregard.

She was dealing with issues of her own, some revolving around my failed marriage to her father, my ex-husband. The added burden of our current stresses was made more difficult for her because at times, I had little energy to spare for anything beyond trying to put one foot in front of the other.

For a time, she became increasingly disrespectful towards me. Once, she actually kicked me, hard. I immediately let her know in no uncertain terms that was totally unacceptable, and restrained her from repeating her actions. She was less than impressed, but I got my message across.

Sometime after that, it became apparent that I needed surgery. My daughter was horrified that she might have been the cause. Of course, she wasn't to blame and I did my best to ease her conscience.

Even so, I think she learned to control her outbursts a bit better after that.

The impending surgery meant that the care of the house and my son would fall to my husband, at least for the time I was in the hospital.

Every day, after my surgery, my daughter came to see me. During one visit, she asked me to move over in the hospital bed so that she could curl up with me, and promptly fell asleep. It wasn't until she woke up that I found out her father was sitting in his truck in the parking lot waiting for her.

My first few days at home were difficult. Not only was I nervous about sharing a bed with my husband, an extremely restless sleeper, I discovered that my daughter had been pressed into service cooking the evening meal.

My husband's reasoning was that this freed him to look after our son.

For the next few days, as soon as my daughter left for school, I moved into her room and napped until my boy got up, then took care of him until my husband got up. My daughter would come home from school to find me resting in her room, her brother happily playing with one of her stuffed toys, and my husband just crawling out of bed.

While she started supper, I would shuffle back to my own bed, knowing that my boy was being taken care of. I felt guilty that the bulk of the care would fall on my daughter's shoulders, but I desperately needed the rest. Fortunately, for all, it was only a couple of days until I was again able to take over, and my son was blissfully oblivious to it all.

I believe the only age my son and I worked smoothly together was when he was three. Looking back, it seemed to be the easiest year we spent together. Yes, bedtime was a challenge, as was supper, but there was less stress in that year compared to the rest.

At least where it concerned my son...

On the other hand, my marriage wasn't doing so well. This is another unfortunate but common occurrence in families dealing with this disability. When the care of a child takes up eighteen to twenty hours out of twenty-four, sometimes even the best efforts of both parents aren't enough to stave off the stress of the additional workload.

This was and is my life. I hope those of you striving to cope with any of these same things will know you are not alone.

Another area where I noticed a difference with my boy was toilet training. I understand that there is no set time for children to be trained, and on the surface, my son appeared to follow the norm. However, long after he knew how to use the bathroom – and by long I mean three years, he was going through several changes of clothes a day due to accidents.

The actual training part was easy. The hard part was ensuring his consistency. He would become so engrossed in playing that he would forget he needed to use the bathroom. I put down his reluctance as a phase he was going through.

This phase continued until he was six. He didn't seem to care one way or the other. I would have saved myself a lot of work and frustration if I had left him in pull-ups until he turned eight. Until then, I did an awful lot of laundry.

At times, I was positive he was regressing. He displayed the same attitude towards clean, dry underwear at the age of eight as he did when he was a toddler.

I have since discovered, after years of wondering why my son refused to use the bathroom when necessary, that this is also common with the disability.

> "...night-time bed-wetting (enuresis) and other problems with toilet training plague children with ADHD more than other children..."
>
> Russell A. Barkley, PhD
> Taking Charge of ADHD

This was another piece of information that I had to discover on my own, as no one felt it was important enough to pass along.

Another useful tidbit, not widely known, is the fact that behaviourally, these children are three to four years behind their peers. This, in retrospect, explains a lot.

I would like to clarify here, that the three to four year difference is behavioural, not intellectual. These kids are smarter than the average bear when it comes to academics. They are even in the gifted range in many areas, except, unfortunately, social skills.

> "Their failure to inhibit their feelings as well as other children of the same age makes us see children with ADHD as emotionally immature."
>
> Taking Charge of ADHD

This can create quite a problem with classroom studies, but I'll get into that later.

While juggling the challenges of mealtimes, toilet training, and of course, sleeping, or not sleeping, if you will, I realized that though I simply couldn't work outside the home, even part-time. Since I was an adequate seamstress, however, I could still bring in some much-needed cash. I came up with an idea to make pillows and sell them at the local flea market.

I coerced my daughter and a few of her friends into helping me stuff my creations, and my little business was born. Every Sunday, I would take my wares to the market to sell. My husband wasn't terribly impressed with my efforts, but I made enough cash every week to pay for gas, some groceries, and the occasional extra.

I was bringing in extra money, and I was still able to look after the household and raise my boy. As far as I was concerned, it was a win-win situation.

My loud and often boisterous son entered pre-school when he was four. As his sleep patterns were still unsettled, he was often awake until midnight. Luckily, for me, the only class available started in the afternoon. This made it easier for me to get my son up and ready in time.

Every day, I would ask the teachers how he had fared in class. I was told there were issues with listening and following instructions. He didn't have a problem sharing toys, but he had to be told repeatedly to put them away before starting a different activity.

His biggest challenge was circle time. During this time, everyone sat quietly in a circle and learned the lesson for the day. My son would be fidgeting constantly, standing up, not paying attention, and generally distracting the other children. As my son says now, of a particularly trying session, "It was a grim day…"

I wasn't sure if preschool was actually teaching my son anything. I was more concerned with improving his social skills.

It was already painfully apparent that he was having trouble making friends.

> "A child with ADHD often has serious problems getting along with other children."
>
> Taking Charge of ADHD

Moving to an apartment complex with few children further limited his opportunities to socialize, but even when we spent afternoons at the park, my son was more interested in playing with the gravel than with other children. It's not that he was shy; he just didn't know how to make friends.

> "...children with ADHD are less able to cooperate and share with other children and to make and keep promises regarding the mutual exchange of favours. This is known as *reciprocity* or *social exchange* and it is at the very heart of developing friendships and demonstrating effective interpersonal dealings with others."
>
> Taking Charge of ADHD

ADHD/ODD kids have trouble relating to their peers. They prefer to engage in their style of play, sometimes acting out their favourite video or game. Other children often view this behaviour as weird, or strange.

I have even heard the words "retarded" and "psycho" applied to my son. Well, I can definitely tell you he is neither retarded, nor crazy – though perhaps a little odd around the edges, by other's standards.

Many times, I asked my son's preschool teacher if he might be showing signs of ADHD. The woman that ran the preschool had dealt with many children who exhibited symptoms of the disability and she reassured me that my son wasn't displaying any of the behaviours associated with it. I was assured my son was completely normal – talk about offering false hopes…

When my son graduated from preschool, complete with a little ceremony, the teachers presented each child with a booklet of pictures taken throughout the year. They inscribed our booklet with a note that read, "Thank you for the opportunity to work with your son. It was definitely challenging trying to come up with different activities to keep him interested."

That should have been a first clue right there.

Chapter 5

Education 101

By the time my son entered kindergarten, his socially restricting behaviours were quite apparent, coupled with a more pronounced inability to focus on tasks involving higher concentration, like dressing himself and cleaning his room. This isn't to say that he couldn't do it, just that he couldn't concentrate on the task long enough to complete it.

> "Dr. Mark Stein...demonstrated that children with ADHD have significant delays in development of adaptive functioning. Adaptive functioning includes self-help skills like dressing, bathing, feeding, and toilet training."
>
> Russell A. Barkley, PhD
> Taking Charge of ADHD

I could not ask my son to get dressed and walk away knowing he would do it. It just did not happen. If I wanted him out the door in time for school, and most days that was impossible, I had to help him. If, for some reason, I didn't stay and help, I would return to find him still in his pyjamas, completely focused on whatever toy had caught his attention.

This inability to follow seemingly simple instructions was a major source of frustration for me. It wasn't just the getting dressed...it was everything.

Keeping him in bed at night continued to be a huge problem. I swear I could have beaten him and he *still* would have climbed out of bed. To this day, even with the Melatonin, I have to sit with him until he falls asleep.

I should point out that at the time of this writing my son is eleven years old. Though I love him fiercely, our relationship has always been tempestuous. This is not a journey for the faint of heart. That we have survived together for this long is a testament to my intestinal fortitude, plus the parenting skills I have learned along the way.

I'm sure you are familiar with the phrase, "How many times do I have to tell you?" I heard it often enough while I was growing up, as I'm sure, you have, too. It has been passed down generation to generation from time immemorial.

With an ADHD/ODD child, the telling can translate into upwards of fifty reminders a day for a single desired action. I don't use that phrase anymore. I have developed a quiet, prompting strategy that works much better most of the time.

I have also accepted that in order to focus my son on a task, I often must initiate the task, and then help until the task is completed. Otherwise, it will remain undone.

Cleaning his room is a particular chore that was generally met with complete non-compliance. The main reason was not that he didn't want to clean his room. That was only part of the problem. He simply did not know where to start. As he surveyed the litter of discarded papers mixed into the jumble of toys randomly strewn about, dotted with empty food wrappers from his lunch bag, the task seemed insurmountable.

Again, after your child is diagnosed, you will become privy to a wealth of information, and strategies to help your child focus on larger tasks, but until then....

Now, I don't know about you, but waging a weekly war over cleaning a bedroom is not how I want to spend my time. I have enough battles to fight without adding more to my agenda. Even simple chores like brushing his teeth, or getting him dressed and ready for school each day, could be exhausting ordeals requiring constant supervision and prompting.

This translated into a much larger workload, and to be honest, I resented it. Not only did I have the household chores, I had to help my son with literally everything except playing.

One of the unfortunate challenges associated with rearing a higher needs child is the strain this places on your marriage.

If you have a supportive spouse who is willing to assist with the additional responsibilities, you are indeed fortunate.

Otherwise, the added stress can kill your relationship.

Things might not have been so hard to take had I been able to sleep for a solid seven hours after putting my son to bed, however, I would be the one to get up and put him back to bed every time he awoke. From his birth to the age of seven or eight, he would wake an average of three times a night. He never slept through the night at home until he was nine, and then only barring bad dreams or accidents.

As you might imagine, after eight years of sleep deprivation, it was easy for me to become cranky.

To be honest it is still easy for me to feel on edge and out of sorts. Even though I have the best and most currently available tools and knowledge to deal with my son, and the neighbours, and the school, etc., raising these children exacts a huge emotional toll. At times, I feel much like a rubber band stretched to its breaking point. The least little thing could be all it takes for me to snap.

Since I'm on the subject of emotions, one of the things I have noticed is how the lack of sleep affects my ability to be patient. As long as I manage to get a good night's sleep, I can handle the daily stresses fairly well, and by daily stresses, I mean not only my son, but everything life throws at you any given day.

Let me put this in perspective for you. Now, I am, generally speaking, a very patient soul. It takes a lot to make me blow a gasket, however when you add up years of sleep deprivation, having little respite from the role of primary caregiver, a very demanding, high needs child, and marital difficulties with all the daily drama that entails, you can see how it could take very little to push me over the edge. Some days I felt like a bomb with a very short fuse.

Most families of children who are diagnosed with these disorders have busy, stress-filled, at times, chaotic lives that no one except another parent of these incredible youngsters could hope to comprehend. I have been told by other such parents who have more than one offspring, that had they been blessed with their behavioural child first, they never would have had a second child. Seems I've heard that somewhere before...

I used to think every problem could be dealt with by the use of proper discipline. After all, that was how I raised my daughter and she grew into a responsible, well-rounded adult. However, after living with my son, my outlook and opinions changed drastically.

It's very difficult to understand the thought processes and subsequent behaviours of a child with ADHD/ODD. When you say, "No" to a child without these disabilities he or she will generally subside and grudgingly acquiesce to your suggestions. The same response is not forthcoming from someone like my son.

Seemingly normal requests, like, "Do your homework," "Brush your teeth," and "Eat your supper," can become the trigger that starts World War III. There is no such thing as a normal request.

Every decision is questioned half a dozen times, argued and debated. Alternate endings are supplied and promises made to help change my mind. This scenario is repeated every single time the word "no" is involved. When you have finished explaining for the umpteenth time, not only is your child cranky, you're so hot under the collar you could fry eggs sans stove.

Another trademark many of these children share is the need to vocalize. In other words, they talk nonstop. Have you ever watched the Bugs Bunny cartoon in which Bugs keeps talking constantly? After telling him repeatedly and loudly to "Shut up!" the other character has to physically stem the flow of Bugs' words.

That's my boy. No matter how many times I tell him to be quiet or to stop, he keeps right on going until he finishes what he needs to say.

Like most of these children, he doesn't have to know anything about the chosen subject: he just needs to expound on it. His opinion is very important...not necessarily to you, or his audience, but it is vitally important to him.

These children are incapable of stopping until they have finished their thought, regardless of whether they have been told to be quiet. Their lives could be in jeopardy and they will keep talking. They won't quit until they have gotten out that last word.

Many times my son will start explaining something to me, and continue even if I have to leave the room. Sometimes, I think he talks just to hear the sound of his own voice. There have been times I've heard him talking and asked if he was speaking to me, only to be told "No."

This type of focus is consistent with the disability.

Try to make these children change direction when they are going full steam ahead. It can't be done, verbally. If you want them to stop what they are doing and start something else, especially if they are enjoying themselves, you must often physically redirect them...and that isn't as easy as it sounds.

Gifted, enigmatic and sometimes as hard to pin down as smoke, these children are a bit like the genie in the bottle.

Once you've pulled the cork, you know how hard it is to persuade the genie back in the bottle.

I have found the best way to help my son change his focus is to give him a time limit.

If I want him to go to bed, I give him a countdown so he will become adjusted to the idea that he soon must stop what he is doing. I tell him, "Bedtime in twenty minutes." Then, ten minutes later I remind him, "You only have ten more minutes, then it's time for bed."

This gives him time to readjust his focus, instead of just demanding he stop what he is doing and change direction. Unless you set a time limit, you may as well stand in front of a stampede, gently flapping your hand and saying, "Please stop."

The results would be equally unproductive, as your child will pay you roughly the same attention, as would the stampeding herd. I don't know about you, but the last thing I need is to feel completely trampled at the end of my day.

Chapter 6

Mom Goes Back to School

After my son entered kindergarten, I realised I, too, needed an education. It wasn't until my son had been attending school for a couple of weeks however, that I was forced to sit up and really take notice.

After class one day, his teacher took me aside telling me I should consider putting him on medication. I was flabbergasted! I was angry that she would suggest such a thing. My son didn't need drugs. Who did she think she was?

The following week, she explained my son was having difficulty following directions, and wasn't listening. He was being disruptive, very disrespectful, and acting out. She then told me I should take him to a paediatrician.

I was still smarting over her comment about medication, and wasn't willing to acknowledge that she might be right. As my son's behaviour worsened though, I finally made an appointment to see a specialist.

The specialist pronounced my son too young to be tested, as he was only five, but I was given a flyer from Community Services. One of the programs available was a course entitled, "Handling the Difficult Child, and ADD/ADHD Child." As my son could be classified as 'difficult', and virtually everything I had tried, had failed, I decided to take the course.

For the next six weeks, I spent every Tuesday evening learning ways to help me parent my son. Each week, I would be given homework involving him that required I note any positive changes in his behaviour. I would love to tell you all my problems were solved, but nothing they suggested worked for very long.

One of the lessons was how to put my son to bed. I was told that in order for my son to become accustomed to sleeping in his own room I was to put him to bed, and then leave.

This seemed like an exercise in futility, as this strategy hadn't worked at all well the first time around – but I tried again. The results were about the same this time.

Another trick they offered was a way to ensure good behaviour when we were out shopping.

My son would ask for treats every time I took him to the store with me. Most kids will stop after being told no a few times. Not my son. He would pick what he wanted and carry it around the store, all the while asking me to buy it.

It didn't matter how many times I said, "No," how many time outs I gave him, how many privileges he lost, or how long he was grounded. He kept right on asking, and not in his in-door voice.

This course taught that we should set down clear rules of conduct. On the way to the store, you were to tell your child what was expected, and make him repeat what you had said before entering the store. If he didn't follow the rules, you were to leave the store.

That's all well and good if, when he misbehaves, you are able to leave your child in the care of someone else so that you can complete your shopping. What do you do when you can't?

The army has a saying, "adapt and overcome." As I could rarely leave my son with anyone, yet needed to get the shopping done, I had to adapt the rules to include striking a bargain for a small reward for good behaviour, and overcome any undesirable behaviour by constantly reminding him of the bargain.

It was always interesting to see whether I would be the only parent in our group to admit, "No, it didn't work." Unfortunately, though I was in a group of parents struggling with similar challenges, I was usually the odd man out.

One thing I did learn that has worked over the long term was how to help my son maintain his focus when working on larger tasks. The key is to break the larger assignment into smaller jobs. Instead of telling my son to clean his room, I now ask him to put away his Lego, or tidy up his desk.

Each one of these chores is part of cleaning his room, but they are small enough that he can see a beginning and an end, so he manages to maintain his focus. He still likes it when I help him though, and he accomplishes more when I do.

A major part of the course was learning to adapt strategies to work with your particular circumstances. One of the tools they offered was a weekly/monthly chart, used for rewarding good behaviour.

All the tasks your child needed to do on a daily basis, from Monday to Sunday were listed on the chart. Each completed chore was given a star, and at the end of the day, all the stars were tallied up. Long-range goals could be charted as well simply by increasing the days to weeks, ultimately showing the whole month.

Using this system, the child has a visual record of his accomplishments over the course of the days, weeks, or months, giving him incentive to regulate his behaviour and achieve whatever rewards had been discussed.

ADD and ADHD children respond to this style of reward system quite well. However, if the Oppositional Defiant Disorder is more pronounced, the success rate drops dramatically.

I was facing that problem, although I didn't know it at the time. I just couldn't understand why a strategy would work for a day or two, and then fail.

The only advice the instructor had for me was "you have to be consistent." Oh, gee.

It is one thing to be consistent, and another thing to beat your head against a wall, which is exactly what it felt like I was doing.

Do you remember seeing the silent movie clips in which a young heroine is tied up on the railroad tracks? There she is; bound and gagged with a locomotive barrelling down upon her, helpless to stop what appears to be her imminent death.

That was how I felt every single time I picked up my son from kindergarten. On the outside, I looked like any other parent, but inside I was cringing, waiting for the train wreck.

My son's behaviour had been growing steadily worse, to the point where I was beginning to dread seeing his teacher. The days of calm and polite behaviour were few and far between. I did my best to maintain a positive attitude, hoping against hope that my son would grow out of this phase, and settle into school.

Alas, my hopes were dashed when my son received his first suspension, rapidly followed by his second, and third, in the span of three days. I was at a loss to understand what triggered this horrible behaviour.

Suddenly, my son went from being a disruptive influence in the classroom to a pint-sized version of Freddie Kruger from *Nightmare on Elm Street*. He tried to cut one student with scissors, hit his teacher and another student, and choked a third.

I was devastated, not only by his behaviour, but because his first school milestone, his very first Christmas concert, which should have been a happy event, was not to be. He was not allowed to attend because of his inappropriate behaviour.

I thoroughly concurred; you don't reward bad behaviour, but I was sad for myself, and heartbroken for my son.

After the dust settled, I was informed that the school was trying to place my son in a behavioural class. Unfortunately, that wasn't possible, but they did manage to provide some support. Whenever he acted out in class, he was sent to a behaviour worker for the rest of the day. He also spent half days once a week with this worker, learning how to interact appropriately with his peers.

This wasn't as effective as I had hoped, as he continued to be sent to the principal's office; however, the violent episodes disappeared.

Through all this, I faithfully attended my weekly Tuesday parenting course in hope of learning something to help with my son's non-interaction at Kindergarten. At the same time, I was doing my best to juggle my part-time work, parent my son and manage the household.

In a desperate bid to keep our marriage afloat, my husband and I decided to take a walk on the wild side, hoping it might rekindle some spark. Unfortunately, as with most desperate measures, it ultimately proved to be a band-aid and not any real solution.

You must be thinking I was a glutton for punishment. Here I was with a difficult child, an unhappy home life, shaky finances, and now I attempt to add an active nightlife. I must have looked like a terrier chasing its tail.

I am sure now that my desperate grasping at any straw aggravated my son's problems, though I did my best to hold it all together. Had I been able to step outside my situation, I might have been able to see then what seems so clear now, but hindsight is twenty-twenty.

For the time being, though, my son appeared to be settling in at school. There were no more violent upheavals. He even sang with a special chorus at a thank you luncheon for the school volunteers. It was a very proud moment for me. I'm sure my son didn't feel the same way, but it made my heart glad to see him standing on the stage with his class mates.

Miraculously, he maintained his improved behavioural level for the rest of the school year. I breathed a sigh of relief. I even entertained the hope that he might grow out of those negative behaviours and settle down. Call me "Pollyanna."

Those of you who have never seen this Disney movie may not be familiar with the reference. 'Pollyanna' is the charming tale of a little girl whose amazingly positive attitude completely changes every life she touches. Some people refuse to credit positive thinking with any power to help us make changes for the better, but if I had looked at my situation any other way, I would have hung up my spurs a long time ago.

My son finished Kindergarten without further suspensions and passed into Grade 1. Summer vacation was filled with trips to the lake and the local water park. My boy's behaviour didn't appear to be worsening, and I refused to entertain any thought of the upcoming school term. I firmly tucked away any speculation into my hope chest along with his finger paintings and Mother's Day cards.

The beginning of Grade 1 heralded a big change. Things started out fairly well. He seemed to like his new teacher, and she was experienced handling active children. If my son was having trouble with class work, he was moved to a table in the back of the room for some one-on-one time with the teacher.

This strategy seemed to help, as he usually completed his work, and managed to stay out of the principal's office. Although my son refrained from hitting anyone, he still had verbal outbursts in class, so he continued to see the behaviour worker on a regular basis.

One such outburst landed him in the worker's office.

He told a student that he wanted to shoot one of the teachers. He then told the worker that he wanted to get a gun and shoot the principal, vice principal, the worker and his teacher, so he wouldn't have to go to class.

In discussion with my son's teacher, she indicated that he appeared to be re-enacting violent video games at recess and throughout the day. Both his teacher and I were deeply concerned about his behaviour, and agreed it certainly wasn't appropriate for school.

This style of play had been a major source of disagreement between my husband and me for quite a while. My husband, an avid video game player, spent most evenings glued to his game controller. His idea of minding our son, from the time the baby could sit up unattended, was to plunk the boy on the couch so he could watch Daddy save the world by killing or maiming everything in sight.

I could see the violence and disregard for others creeping into my son's play from an early age, but no matter how often we butted heads over the video game situation, nothing changed. My husband didn't seem to understand that our son was too young to be watching these violent games, no matter how entertaining he found them.

The resulting battles generally ended with two extremely angry parents and nothing resolved. I felt like I was beating my head against a wall.

Upon hearing what had happened at school, and my renewed pleas to refrain from gaming while our son was up, my husband's only response was to tell the boy that he shouldn't act out the games at school.

The video games continued unabated. From the time supper was finished until my son's bedtime, I was constantly removing him to his bedroom to prevent him watching his dad play video and computer games. Can you spell frustration?

Fortunately, his father's explanation that he shouldn't re-enact video games at school seemed to help our son moderate his behaviour. At any rate, he wasn't acting out as much.

Finally, though, the frustrations and stress took their toll. In May 2004, I separated from my husband, took my son and moved to Surrey.

My daughter, who had been living with her father, moved back in with us.

And that was the end of the world, as we knew it.

Chapter 7

The End of the World

I had thought moving out would be bad, but even at its worst, nothing in my married life had prepared me for the shock of my new life. Good days were awful: bad days seemed as if the doors of hell had been thrown wide and the apocalypse was upon us.

As if the Powers That Be were foretelling what life would be like in our new home, our move there was the worst I have ever experienced. The rental company double booked, leaving us without a moving van. Everyone I had asked to help bailed at the last minute. Once I finally rounded up a truck for the day and made the thirty-minute drive to drop off our first load, we discovered our new suite still occupied and unavailable until the next day.

The following day, we started again. We couldn't get in until the landlord brought a key for the suite, but I couldn't sit there and wait for him. We had to keep bringing loads or we would be at it all night. With only the two of us to load and unload, we were forced to leave all our belongings unattended in the back yard. We moved five pickup loads before he arrived.

Finally, we were able to transfer everything into the suite. It wasn't until we had moved in half the furniture that we discovered my son's bike had been stolen.

Was this an indication of things to come?

We settled in as best we could. My son liked the neighbourhood, met the kids in the area, and even learned to ride a bike without training wheels. He had coerced one of the neighbourhood kids into lending his bike, and proceeded to show me how well he could ride...without training wheels. That was a huge step for my son, and I was very proud of his accomplishment. I vowed to buy him a new bike as soon as I could. Finally all seemed to be going well.

Anyone who has been through a marital breakup, though, understands the devastation children experience. Overnight their world is turned upside down, but they are expected to continue as if nothing has happened. Because we are forced to be adults and go on about our lives, we can lose sight of what our children are experiencing unless something brings it to our attention.

I didn't have long to wait.

Within the first week in his new classroom, my son had intimidated his teacher to the point that she let him do almost anything he wanted. If he didn't feel like doing his work, he didn't. In only one month, my son's unruly behaviour escalated to the point that the school sent him home regularly.

Here's how it went…

As part of the school curriculum, my son's class took swimming lessons at the local pool. He made it through four lessons before being banned from the pool for bad behaviour.

Then the phone calls started. "Could you please come and pick up your son." His teacher had no idea how to handle him, so her solution was to send him to the office. They in turn didn't know what to do, so they followed suit, and called me to pick him up.

In the space of three weeks, my son went from attending full days, to attending no more than an hour. Every day I would walk him to school, and every day I would pray I wouldn't get a phone call. Some days I would just get in the door and the phone would ring. I began to dread the sound.

My son was acting out so badly, in part, because of the separation. I did my best to talk to him about it, and ensured he saw his father every other weekend, but that didn't seem to be enough. I suggested changing the weekend schedule from bi-weekly to every weekend in the hopes that would give my son more stability.

Of course, when my son was sent home, there were consequences. He was grounded to his room for the duration of the school day. TV and video games were out of the question. He was allowed to read, or play with his Lego until the regular dismissal time, but even then, no games or television until after supper.

Yes, I had to make sure there were consequences for his actions, but I soon reached the point where I felt I was not only punishing him, I was punishing myself.

One morning after dropping my son at school, I walked in the door at home, and the phone was ringing. "Come pick up your son please," so off I went back to get him. The principal was waiting for me, and I asked her "Why should I even bother bringing him?"

She replied, "The interaction is good for him."

Excuse me? I looked at her and said, "He's here for fifteen minutes a day, what kind of interaction is that?" Then I turned around, leaving her standing there with her mouth open, collected my boy and left.

Shortly after that, my son started seeing the school counsellor. After a few sessions, the counsellor called me in to see him. He asked several questions about my son, and mentioned that there was a possibility that he could get support at school, but my son's behaviour would have to be evaluated first.

In the final month of school, his teachers were asked to complete The Problem Behaviour Questionnaire, the Hawthorne EBPS-2 Home Version Rating Form, and the Conner's Teacher Rating Scale (Profile for Males).

I was given the Conner's Parent Rating Scale (Profile for Males) to fill out.

Though the test results showed exceptionally high for ADHD, they were only an indication. The clinical diagnosis could only be made by a medical professional.

Two days after school finished for the year, and my son was promoted into Grade 2, he was finally seen by a paediatrician who prescribed twenty milligrams sustained release Ritalin for ADHD.

Once I came to grips with the guilt inspired by the fact my son needed medication, I imagined that Ritalin would be a cure-all for the effects of the ADHD.

It was not.

I started my son's summer treatment with a positive attitude. I thought now that we had Ritalin, everything would begin to settle down, however, that was not in the cards.

My son was still struggling with the fact that his father no longer lived with us. This caused increasingly rebellious behaviour, most of it directed towards me, in the form of rude comments, open defiance, bad manners, and destructive actions.

Plastic lawn chairs began turning up broken. Of course, not one neighbourhood kid owned up to it, mine included. The siding on the corner of the house began disappearing; my car became a jungle gym; and a collection of tree branches miraculously appeared on my back porch.

> "These conduct problems can progress to more severe forms of antisocial behaviour such as lying, stealing, fighting, running away from home, destroying property, and other delinquent or criminal behaviour..."
>
> Russell A. Barkley, PhD
> Taking Charge of ADHD

To be honest, the vehicle was quite an eyesore and didn't look driveable, but that wasn't the issue. I offered restitution, and it was accepted, thank goodness. Needless to say, my son was grounded, again.

> "It is common for parents to resort to punishment when a child misbehaves or disobeys. This may be all right for a child without ADHD, who misbehaves only occasionally...it is not all right for a child with ADHD, who is likely to misbehave much more often..."
>
> Taking Charge of ADHD

It made little difference whether he was grounded, though. I discovered shortly after that incident, that my son would climb out his window and sneak into the adjacent park to play.

Looking back, I have to give my son credit for his cleverness, however at the time, I was mad as hell.

One beautifully sunny afternoon, as I was relaxing in the backyard, the next-door neighbour stopped by the fence and cleared his throat. I could tell this was not to be a friendly conversation from his crossed arms and the scowl on his face.

Before I even had a chance to say "Hello," he put his hands on the fence and demanded, "Is there something wrong with your son?"

"Yes, there is," I replied. "He has ADHD/ODD, Anxiety Disorder, and some Post Traumatic Stress. Do you have a solution for me?"

My candour completely took the wind out of his sails. The man took a step back, his mouth working. He looked like a beached fish. After a couple of seconds, he apologised, and started talking to me normally. Score one for Mom. At that point, I was willing to take any victory, no matter how small.

My son soon developed the rather nasty habit of throwing his dinner out the window when he didn't want to eat. This persisted for two years despite groundings, time outs, spankings, and loss of privileges.

I felt like I was losing control.

When placed in the charge of his now eighteen-year-old sister, he fought with her constantly, kicking and punching her, and refusing to heed her. His behaviour grew so out of control that she refused to look after him.

He also started swearing.

Now, I know all kids begin exercising that freedom when out of earshot of their parents, but he was taking it to a new level. I wonder how many of the parents reading this recall their first taste of soap. It's not something one forgets. I know my son won't. Yet despite that deterrent, he persisted.

He pushed everything well past the limit. Whether he was refusing to come in when I called, making rude comments, breaking his toys, or simply not wanting to brush his teeth, he made everything a chore. There wasn't one day that went by that we didn't wage at least one battle.

By the end of summer, I hadn't seen much change in my son's behaviour. I couldn't tell if the meds were working. They obviously didn't have any effect on his attitude, which was worsening every day. His sleeping habits hadn't changed, and his appetite was dwindling. I had expected the move and separation to cause some deterioration, but I had expected nothing like this.

A week before school started, I received a phone call from the school board regarding my son's placement for Grade 2. In answer to requests for help, my son was to be admitted to a school that had a behavioural program. I was elated! Finally, we were going to get the proper support, and my boy would be able to attend school regularly.

At the time, I didn't realize how bad my son's behaviour was going to become.

Chapter 8

Crime and Punishment

We started the school year with a positive, hopeful attitude. At least I started that way. My son, on the other hand, wasn't thrilled about going to school at all. While he was meeting his teacher and classmates, I was meeting with the teacher's aides, childcare workers, principal, and head of the division for the behavioural program.

We put an Individual Behaviour Plan (IEB) together, making a note of a future psychiatric assessment appointment, as requested by my son's Grade 1 guidance counsellor. The plan was to be discussed again in three months, to see where he was behaviourally and academically.

My son started school at recess, and stayed until lunchtime. Now, though, instead of being sent home immediately, he was taken to the behavioural home room, where he could work on his own, cool down if necessary, and eat lunch.

We hoped this strategy would be enough to fully integrate him into the classroom on a full-time basis.

After the three-month evaluation, they had a better understanding. Here are their findings:

"Behavioural Strengths – is spending most of the school day in the regular classroom with good success, likeable and friendly, has made friends in the classroom, sense of humour.

Areas of Concern – has violent tendencies (re-enacts video game behaviour and sound effects,) fixates on behaviours and has trouble with transitions, is physically abusive to adults when plans change, needs to develop self monitoring behaviour.

Long Term Goal – to integrate full time into the regular classroom, to reduce violent mimicking behaviour (i.e. shooting stabbing, blowing up sound effects), to be outside at recess/lunch, to reduce physically abusive reactions to change in routine or not getting what he wants.

Academic – very strong academically, is able to complete all assignments with good results, very neat and capable worker.

No areas of Concerns at this time.

Long Term Goal – to fully meet expectations for the Grade 2 program in all subject areas as well as social responsibilities.

Short Term Objectives – to integrate from recess to the end of the day with NO outbursts in the regular classroom, to eliminate video sound effects during recess and lunch breaks, replace negative language, to express his feelings in a more positive way."

They had their work cut out for them. I have been trying since pre-school to stop the video game behaviour with no success to date.

I even had the teachers backing when I now asked his father to limit the amount of time our son watched the violent games, and asked that he no longer be allowed to play them.

Unfortunately, I couldn't monitor that anymore, so I had to take his father's word. I even collaborated with my mother-in-law to try to stop the video violence. It was an ongoing battle.

When report cards were issued in December, his was optimistic. He seemed to be settling in without any further outbursts. Unfortunately, on December 14, after two days of verbal abuse, hair pulling, kicking and hitting, as I later heard, my son was suspended until after the winter break. So much for optimism…

My son was to spend that Christmas week with his father and grandparents, so I jumped at the invitation to visit my sisters in Alberta, and run away from home for a few days.

I spent the holiday doing absolutely nothing. My sisters were concerned that I would be bored, as they had to work while I was there, but their fears were unfounded. A whole week of no responsibilities, no fights, no cooking or cleaning, just peace and quiet – I was in heaven. Looking back on it now, I believe it was one of the best Christmases I ever had.

The New Year brought with it another two suspensions. The first was because my son punched a Child Care Worker in the stomach, and the second was because he attempted to stab the Child Care Worker with scissors, kicked and hit the worker, pulled the worker's hair, and was threatening students in his class with scissors and pencils.

What a great way to start the year!

In mid January, an intake referral to the Child and Youth Mental Health office was made, citing "...behaviours which are of concern and which appear to be increasing in severity and frequency..." as the reason behind the referral.

> "Many of these defiant children are also aggressive towards others. They may be quick to get angry, verbally attack others, or even physically assault others..."
>
> Russell A. Barkley, PhD
> Taking Charge of ADHD

At the end of January, I was called in to discuss a Safety Plan for my son, due to escalating undesirable behaviour. The objective was "...to ensure that staff working with (my son) are aware of staff responses and safety procedures in place to maintain a safe, productive learning environment for (my son), other students and staff." They then listed the key understandings about my son:

"He is a bright and capable student, strengths – reading, neatness, artistic, - very defiant about anything he doesn't want to do, very explosive – physically aggressive against adults, needs a quiet space to calm down (20 – 30 minutes)"

The behaviours listed in the safety plan fell into three categories: anxiety, defensive, and acting out, each with a corresponding response. In order, the prescribed responses were: "be supportive, be directive, and crisis intervention".

The situation looked pretty scary when you realized the whole plan was created to control a seven year old. However, at the time, my son would stop listening, cover his ears when spoken to, say, "I hate you" to classmates and staff, threaten staff; demand to go home; stare at the staff, maintaining direct eye contact to intimidate; threaten to hit or kill the staff; and hit or kick them.

Grade 2 was not going well.

Of course, when I was informed about each suspension, or had to pick up my son from school early because of his behaviour – a task that I performed on a regular basis – I had the opportunity to speak with his teachers and workers.

I did notice that the people associated with my son were, with one exception, all women. My son already had a great deal of anger towards the main woman in his life, me, over the separation from his father.

As well, not one of the staff ever spoke to my son firmly, or with conviction. Every one of them, including the principal, spoke in soft, modulated tones, and used calm reasoning to try to stop my son's rampaging behaviour.

Using that approach with my son is like smiling calmly at a charging rhinoceros, while politely asking that it cease and desist.

I believe, however, if they had spoken to my son in firm, no-nonsense tones they would have achieved much better results. It wouldn't have worked every time, but there might have been fewer incidents if they had.

My son knew that he intimidated the staff. He didn't care that he was sent home: he didn't like school. Sending him home was, to him, the same as handing over the keys to the candy store with an all-you-can-eat coupon.

> "Despite the overall effectiveness of punishment, some unpleasant side effects may occur...effects include the escalation of the problem behaviour, the child's dislike of the teacher, or (in rare cases) the avoidance of school altogether."
>
> Taking Charge of ADHD

On February 2nd, my son and I consulted the referring psychiatrist. The resulting diagnosis was Oppositional Defiant Disorder, Attention-Deficit/Hyperactivity Disorder, Anxiety Disorder, and some Post Traumatic Stress. There it was, in the open.

Finally, some of my son's behaviours made sense.

> "Up to 45% of children with ADHD have a least one other psychiatric disorder besides ADHD, and many have two or more additional disorders. Children with ADHD also display more symptoms of anxiety and depression that do not qualify for a formal psychiatric diagnosis than do other children."
>
> Taking Charge of ADHD

That didn't make them easier to live with. Knowing what causes the behaviour doesn't do much for the daily wear and tear on the nerves. When my son said or did something deliberately, my first thought was not, "Oh it's the disability..." I still reacted and grew angry.

The reality of dealing with the disabilities as opposed to bad behaviours didn't set in for quite a while. I still faced the same behaviours; the only difference was now they had a clinical name - disabilities. Understanding why the behaviours occur, though, and finding ways to handle them takes time.

We all would like to believe once you know what you are dealing with, everything is easier – instant diagnosis, instant fix. That is not the reality of the situation.

I know – I made that same mistake. I thought now that my son's problems were labelled, his teachers would know how to handle him. I was lulled by the fact that he was in a behavioural program. There were other children enrolled in the program, and the teachers and aides had been trained to deal with the challenges these kids brought to the table, however, they hadn't been faced with anyone like my son.

The day after the assessment, my son was suspended for threatening physical abuse to a number of students in his class…another reality check.

> "Punishment when used alone or in the relative absence of ongoing rewards and positive feedback is not very effective at changing behaviour."
>
> Taking Charge of ADHD

In March of that year, my son received two more suspensions — once for knocking two of his classmate's heads together and the second for hitting the Social Development teacher from behind with a full backpack.

I remember that day well. He wasn't allowed to ride the school bus home, and I had to pick him up from the office. When I found out why, I looked in his backpack. It contained his daily folder with two sheets of paper in it, two pencils, and a half sandwich from his lunch. This constituted a full backpack.

Don't misconstrue what I am saying here. Yes, my son was at fault. Yes, it was legitimate grounds for being sent home. And yes, it most likely hurt. What I haven't told you is the teacher went on to claim ongoing back problems caused being hit from behind with a full backpack.

We made it through the rest of March and almost half way through April before he received another suspension. I was called to the school to collect my son, and was told that my son had kicked the Child Care Worker in the leg twenty-three times.

I was astounded! The worker laughed at my shocked expression and told me he had made a game out of it to diffuse the attack.

Looking him in the eyes I said, "You made a *game* out of my son kicking you? Just what is that teaching him: that it's okay to kick somebody?"

He explained that they had been trying to restrain my son without hurting him. I told him about an alternate method, similar to the "Stop" gesture that traffic officers use, and demonstrated for him, quickly thrusting my hand, palm out within a few inches of his nose while firmly saying, "Stop." He took a hasty step back.

I told him this method was in no way abusive, and wouldn't hurt my boy, as there was no physical contact involved, but it would definitely divert him from kicking.

I couldn't help wondering what the WCB personnel would think, if my son's worker had ever filed a report about this. "Reason for claim: being kicked in the leg twenty-three times."

I was told, after the incident, that in fact there had been four injury claims made involving my son's actions.

Chapter 9

a Fox in the Henhouse

Two weeks later, I was called to the school. By this time, I was so resigned to the phone calls I was answering the phone with, "I'll be there shortly." Imagine my surprise when, after I arrived, I was ushered into a room with my son's Child Care Worker and two total strangers.

The strangers introduced themselves as Child Welfare Workers, and explained that my son had disclosed to his worker that he was the victim of ongoing sexual abuse.

You could have knocked me over with a feather! For the next hour and a half, I was grilled about our home life, my ex-husband, friends, neighbourhood families, and the kids my son played with.

When they were finished, I felt like a wrung-out dishrag.

To top it off, my son received another suspension for a period of not less than 5 days for "Escalating violence towards staff members and other students. There is a concern for the safety of others when (my son), in his present state, is at school."

The principal of the school sent a suspension report to the school board, containing a description of my son's suspensions, and ended the report with these comments.

"(My son) has been in an increasingly agitated state and we are concerned for the safety of staff and other students. (See reports) It seems to me, that before we can begin to work with him on social issues and anger management, he must feel safe. With the recent disclosure of sexual abuse and the ongoing exposure to his abuser, we are feeling at a loss to help him. I am concerned that as he spirals out of control, our staff and students are at risk of further injury. We are seeking support for him to begin to deal with his outside issues before he returns to school. We are seeking a meeting of all involved parties."

I received a letter the next day regarding his suspension. As well, I was informed that I would be contacted to arrange a meeting as soon as possible to resolve the suspension. I was given the District Resource Counsellor's name and phone number if I had any questions. I had a bad feeling about this.

During this ordeal, I had put in a referral to Child Mental Health for an outside counsellor, and followed up several times. However, due to a backlog of applications, my son was not scheduled for an intake meeting until the end of May.

I was contacted two days later by the District Resource Counsellor, and told a meeting was arranged for May 4th. I used the ten days trying to get to the bottom of the sexual abuse, which my son now vehemently denied.

I should explain here, that another trait common to these children is their uncanny ability to fabricate a story on the spot. Sometimes this occurs in response to being asked why they are acting out. Whatever the stimulus, they seem instinctively able to tell of an actual or imagined incident in a way guaranteed to cause the most possible upset in any given situation.

> "Often lies...to obtain items or favours or to avoid debts or obligations (i.e., "cons" other people)...
>
> Russell A. Barkley, PhD
> Taking Charge of ADHD

I finally discovered that the party involved was the young teenage son of my neighbour, and I immediately spoke to the child's mother. Fortunately, the alleged abuse was only boys being boys – you show me yours; I'll show you mine – and no touching or explicit sexual acts of any type were committed.

I explained what had happened at my son's school to the boy's mother. I ensured that my son was never alone with the boy, and cut off any visits to his house, though, as we lived in the same four-plex, it was difficult to avoid him all together. I also told the boy what I knew. Yes, the boy's behaviour had been totally unacceptable, but I felt I had dealt with the incident appropriately.

The Child Welfare Workers paid a visit to my home, and we discussed my findings. At first, they advocated for prosecution, but finally accepted my decision and closed the file.

I was satisfied my son was not at risk, and I simply had too much to deal with. I couldn't face adding more.

By this time, my ex-husband's behaviour towards me had deteriorated from merely uncooperative and obstructive to downright abusive.

I had a determinedly delinquent seven-year-old son and a hormonal nineteen-year-old daughter who fought constantly with each other, no support, and no relief in sight.

The last thing I wanted was to drag my son through lengthy battles with the police and the courts. We were already going through enough, and I knew this wouldn't help.

Around this same time, my daughter decided to move out.

Our living arrangement had been simple. As she didn't drive at the time, I had spent the past year taxiing her to and from public transportation so that she could finish college, get to work, and visit her friends. Although she did contribute towards groceries, she didn't pay rent, and flatly refused anything to do with her brother's care. Still, it was nice to have someone to talk to those rare times she was both at home and in a civil mood.

She had been doing respite care for a family, as well as working part-time since finishing college, and dealing with her own emotional problems throughout all of this. Now, she decided to accept the family's offer to move in with them.

In answer to my repeated queries of, "What's wrong? Why haven't I heard from you?" she finally replied via email that I was a horrible person, and lousy mother. She let me know she felt that I was to blame for her brother's behaviour, and that I should be more responsible instead of trying to "foist him off on a babysitter" a couple of hours a week so that I could have a break.

Such is the life of a mother to endure the judgements of her offspring, but I was still mad enough to spit nickels.

May 4th, my son and I met with his principal, the Social Development teacher, the head of the behavioural program, and the Resource Counsellor. It was decided, after much discussion, that my son would be expelled from the school, and my only recourse would be to enrol him in the Success Maker Program, an online, in-home school. Just what I wanted: to add full-time teacher to my list of daily activities.

> "School staff members often may be too quick to let parents take over academically related responsibilities, to the detriment of family life and the parent-child relationship."
>
> Taking Charge of ADHD

Though his suspensions had shown me how hard it would be to home school him full-time, I had no other option. Within two days, I had enrolled my son in the program, and tackled the completion of his Grade 2 education.

I also was successful in obtaining an outside counsellor for my son, and he was seeing her once a week. By the end of the month, my son had completed the program and started his summer holidays.

Considering everything we had been through this school year, I decided that it wasn't in our best interests to stay where we were. I felt it would be better for my boy to be in a smaller town, closer to his father and grandparents.

After careful deliberation, I gave our landlord notice, my daughter and I parted company, and my son and I moved to Mission.

I needed to find a school better suited to my son's needs. I know he had acted horribly towards the faculty and in smaller measure towards the kids in his class, but the strategies used to control him were ineffectual, to say the least.

All they did was teach him that he only had to act outrageously and he would be sent home. He wasn't learning the proper skills, either socially or academically.

True, I was having difficulty managing him at home, but I could only pray that, with this move, my time in purgatory was finally over.

Chapter 10

Location, location

We managed to find a suitable basement suite in Mission with plenty of kids in the area for my son to play with.

> "If your child has already begun hanging out with a deviant, aggressive, or antisocial peer group, do your best to sever her relationship...give serious attention to moving to a different neighbourhood... Research actually shows that moving to a new community and exposing your child to more appropriate peers can do a lot to decrease her risk of delinquency and antisocial activities."
>
> Russell A. Barkley, PhD
> Taking Charge of ADHD

I was delighted to find a school within walking distance, and promptly enrolled my son.

From my first meeting with the principal, I was very clear about my expectations. I related what had transpired at the last school, and told them that my son needed a different type of discipline, and if this school couldn't handle him, I needed help finding one that could.

Further, I explained that I had no intention of home schooling my boy, so I refused to accept sending my son home as a disciplinary action.

Fortunately, the principal agreed with me. He felt that all children should have the opportunity to enjoy the school environment, and didn't see a problem working with my boy.

I can't tell you how refreshing it was to hear that after the way he had been handled in the behavioural program.

Moving to a different town meant that my son had to transfer to another psychologist. This was good, though, because the transfer enabled my boy to see a counsellor much sooner, rather than starting over with an intake meeting. The new counsellor wouldn't be able to see my son until school started, but that was still sooner than waiting for a new intake.

We spent the summer getting settled and exploring the area. We were still close enough to go to all our familiar places, and we added a few new ones. My son seemed to enjoy our new home, which, for someone who hated change, was a big step. However, I still had to see how school would pan out, and I wasn't naive enough to think there would be no challenges along the way.

One such challenge that would be off the list this year though, was my son's principal. For the first time since my son started school, I had found someone willing to help. Not only did this principal agree that my son should be in school, he also agreed that my boy shouldn't serve out-of-school suspensions.

Instead of using that as a deterrent, he would use in-school suspensions and detentions. If my son decided not to listen to his teacher or proved to be too difficult to handle, he would be removed from the classroom and work one on one with his aide. If he didn't complete his work by the end of the school day, he would be kept in until he did.

After so many years of frustration, I was thrilled with what I was hearing, though I was doubtful they would follow through.

Still, they seemed to care that my son received an education.

> "Suspension from school (usually from one to three days) is sometimes used as punishment for severe behaviour problems, but it should be used with much caution. Many children may find staying at home or full-day daycare more enjoyable than being in school."
>
> Taking Charge of ADHD

I have noticed over the years that mothers of these enigmatic children have to fight tooth and nail for their offspring's rights. If these children had a visible disability, there would be no problem in achieving the treatment for them as for any other disabled child. However, since they look exactly the same as normal children, it is very difficult for teachers, neighbours, other parents, and peers to grasp that these children have a disability.

Even when people accept there is a disability, they don't understand all that is involved. It can take years of working with these kids to be able to comprehend what they and their families go through on a daily basis, and the kind of supports they require.

I highly recommend for any parent or teacher of an ADHD/ODD child the book, *Taking Charge of ADHD – The Complete, Authoritative Guide for Parents* by Russell A. Barkley, PhD. *Revised 2005, Guilford Press.*

By the time I was introduced to this book, I had already discovered much of Barkley's findings through living with my son and adapting to his needs. I was, however, most pleased to be validated on many aspects. Things that I had been trying to explain to family and friends for years were stated in black and white. These things were not figments of my overheated mind...they were verifiable facts.

That doesn't mean it became a cure-all for my son's behaviour, but the book does offer some steps to dealing with the daily stress.

The first day of Grade 3 went well. It was a part day, and not structured, so there was little stress. Day two was a bit more challenging.

This particular school starts each new school year by having the students report to their previous year's classroom. This way, the staff can see how many students they have, and decide where to put them all. My son did not know this, not having attended there before, so, on the second day, when the teachers moved him to a new classroom with a different teacher, he dug in his heels.

Not exactly an auspicious beginning.

Within a week, I had my first of many care team meetings with my son's teacher, the school counsellors, and the principal. I filled out an IBP (Intense Behaviour Profile), which allowed my son to have a teacher's assistant in the classroom. We discussed solutions to several of the many challenges they would be facing in the coming weeks, agreeing to meet again in a month.

On September 16, 2005, my son received his first suspension, for being disrespectful and defiant towards his teacher and teacher's assistant. He was sent home for a day, but the principal used a professional development day for the out-of-school suspension. That way, my son didn't lose any class time.

When he returned to school on the Monday, he was told he would be staying after school until all his work was finished – a refreshing change of pace from previous disciplinary actions.

My son managed to keep it together for just over a month. On October 26, he received his second suspension, this time for telling his Teacher's Assistant he was going to rip her head off.

I was called in for another care team meeting. More solutions were set down, one being the "1, 2, 3 approach". This is simple, and I'm sure there are many parents who use the same principal.

For those who are unfamiliar with this principal, the child is asked to do something...if he doesn't comply, he is told, "1", if he still resists, he is told, "2" usually he doesn't have to be told "3" because the child has learned if he hears "3" he has either lost a privilege or something worse.

The school took it one-step further, and made a physical manifestation of the steps. They placed three blocks on the teacher's desk. If, after being given a directive, my son refused to comply, or his behaviour wasn't modified to within acceptable levels, he lost a block.

After he lost three blocks and still refused the task, he was moved to the back of the room to work. If that failed, he was removed from the room to a supervised quiet area.

The duration of class time was regulated as well, to accustom my son to the classroom by gradually increasing the length of time he was expected to control his behaviour. He started by attending school for only two hours a day, from morning bell to recess, then he was excused.

His teacher structured her class so that any social activities like music and gym were held after recess. This ensured that he would receive actual schoolwork, and lessened the chance of a social overload.

After my son had shown he was interested, and capable of more interaction, his attendance would be increased. This was charted daily by the teacher's aide, and a group meeting was held every two to three months to discuss his progress.

By November of that year, his time had increased to half a day. However, ten days later, he received another suspension, for being defiant. Clearly, though he hadn't been exhibiting the violent behaviour that permeated his Grade 2 attendance, we still had a long way to go.

When my son's class time was extended, another strategy was brought into play. After he lost all three blocks, and didn't respond to the final step of supervised quiet time, he was removed to the principal's office to continue his schoolwork. If that failed, he served an in-school suspension.

This entailed staying in the principal's office after the regular dismissal time for whatever length was deemed fitting. The idea was to counteract his learned behaviour of acting out in order to go home.

In-school weekly counselling was also set in place. This was to help him debrief, and talk through any challenges or upsets that occurred during the week.

My next step was to request a Community Service Worker to help him with his social behaviour.

> "By following a preventive regimen, you catch problems before they get too serious, so we advocate establishing a relationship with a professional – a psychologist, physician, or social worker – with whom you meet periodically to review your adolescent's progress."
>
> Taking Charge of ADHD

The worker took my son out into the community once a week, and helped him adapt his social skills. One problem that was addressed in this way was grocery shopping, for which I am still grateful.

Altogether, my son had three counselling sessions a week, one in school, one in the community, and one at a psychologist's office. This may sound excessive, but given his defiant, disruptive behaviour, I felt it was warranted.

My son's counsellor referred him to a registered psychologist for an assessment report. He was concerned about my son's anxiety issues and his advanced vocabulary. He referred my son for a standardized assessment of "his current cognitive and socio-emotional functioning to assist with treatment recommendations."

I have to admit to being confused by all the terminology.

It was frustrating, wading through the myriad of tests, assessments, reports, and care team meetings, in triplicate. I felt as if I had been filling out some kind of form at least once a month, since my son's diagnosis.

There is no rest from the responsibility. Unless you are living it, you really have no idea of the duality of this kind of life. On the one hand, you are totally in love with your child, but on the other, you wish you could sell him to the first band of gypsies to pass your way.

This love/hate relationship is normal. It is also one of the most confusing aspects of raising these children. Part of the time, you function well

– an amazing parent with enormous amounts of patience and love. At other times, you berate yourself for the frustration and anger you feel towards your child. You begin to feel trapped and alone.

This can become a vicious circle.

Grappling with the "I love you – I hate you" duality, beating yourself up with recriminations and self-hatred, you can easily slide into the downward spiral of clinical depression.

One of the most important things you can do for yourself at this stage is to find a support group.

You truly are not alone in your struggles. There are many support associations available for parents of ADHD children throughout Canada and the United States. There are also a number of smaller community based or regional groups. Your local Community Services should have a list of organizations that can help.

As the contacts for these groups change frequently, it is best to get in touch with one of the national organizations. They maintain current records for many of the various local support groups, and can refer you to the ones closest to you.

The largest national organization is CHAAD, Children and Adults with Attention-Deficit/Hyperactivity Disorder. There are more than five hundred support association affiliates from almost every province and state.

> "Maybe the last thing you want to do when you need to be reinvigorated is meet with a group of people who have the same problems you do, but attending support group meetings regularly has multiple benefits."
>
> Taking Charge of ADHD

Your Community Services should also have a program or counsellor available for one on one support.

Unfortunately, I wasn't given this information until much later in my son's school career. The only resource that was brought to my attention was personal counselling. That suggestion seemed to lay even more guilt at my feet, implying that I was the root of my son's problems. I felt personal counselling was not a viable option for me at that time. I had enough on my plate already, and I've never been one to discuss my problems with a total stranger in the hope it will make me feel better.

  I didn't need to feel better. I needed solutions.

Chapter 11

a Glimmer of Hope

I've been told that when you take inspired action, miracles are possible.

Most of my son's success in school to date is due, in part, to my advocacy, and as well, to the wonderful, committed professionals who shaped his Grade 3 experience: his teacher, who unfortunately retired after completing that school year, his teacher's aide, and his principal, who never faltered in his conviction that my son could be successful within the school system.

When we moved to Mission, I couldn't know there was a place less than five minutes away that would help my son claw his way back from the brink of delinquency. I simply knew I had to find a school that could not only handle my boy, but would be willing to help him develop his potential – a tall order considering my son's prior school record, his disabilities, and his behaviour…and what is it they say about three strikes?

I didn't harbour any illusions about my son's willingness to participate in school. As well, I had witnessed the actions of trained professionals in two other schools, so I was holding my breath while interviewing this newest, potential principal.

After speaking with him for ten minutes, I was stunned. The man was amazing!

If you have stepped inside an elementary school, you will know that it is impossible to carry on a conversation without being interrupted at least twice, especially if you happen to be speaking to the principal.

No matter who momentarily distracted him from our conversation, he treated everyone to a pleasant "hello," and a feeling of importance. His greetings were sincere, as was his assurance to see them when we were finished.

I was impressed.

I felt the same way about my son's new teacher. She was genuinely concerned about his grade levels in math and spelling, and restructured her teaching schedule so that that he could catch up to the rest of his class.

The teacher's assistant assigned to help my son was one of the most gracious individuals I had ever met. Rain or shine, sick or healthy, she maintained a cheerful, positive demeanour, despite whatever behaviour my son exhibited.

This woman was no pushover. She handled his outbursts in a calm, firm manner, but was quick to celebrate his victories, no matter how small. She charted his daily progress in the classroom for our bi-monthly meetings, and offered her insights regarding disciplinary measures, and rewards.

With a student counsellor, the Community Services counsellor, and the Child Mental Health counsellor on board, I felt we finally had a team of professionals committed to helping my son.

All of these things fell into place because I zigged when I would have zagged, and decided to look beyond familiar neighbourhoods for our new home.

His November Psychological Assessment showed that, overall, he scored very high in many of the areas tested:

> Verbal comprehension – 86% - Average/Superior
> Perceptual reasoning – 95% - High average/Gifted
> Working memory – 75% - Average/High average
> Processing speed – 66% - Average/High average
> Reading: 97% - Grade 8 level
> Math: 34% - Grade 2 level
>
> "...this is not surprising as his score on working memory and processing speed were significantly lower than his scores in verbal comprehension."
>
> Spelling: 55% - Grade 2 level
>
> Behavioural observations: "...he required consistent encouragement and persuasion

> to continue working...he needed several breaks during the 2 hour session, and asked to see his counsellor several times...generally he was confident and pleasant."

It was as well that our life was beginning to look up on the school front, as we had still a long way to go in so many other ways.

Shortly after his November assessment, I received my first visit from the R.C.M.P.

It wasn't unusual to see police cruisers in the neighbourhood. I lived at the upper end of an area known as a hot spot for domestic disputes.

Imagine my surprise, however, when I answered a knock at *my* door to see a police constable standing on the step. I immediately concluded that he was there because of my son. Unfortunately, I was right.

It transpired that my son had been playing with some kids down the street and left his handheld video game in their house. When he went to retrieve it, he wasn't allowed in. He tried to get the kids to find his game, but they refused, shut the door in his face and locked it.

When knocking on the door didn't produce a parent for my son to speak to, he resorted to kicking. That garnered results, but not the one he was looking for.

The mother assumed my son was unbalanced, which, by this time, he was, barricaded herself in the kitchen, and phoned the police.

Enter the R.C.M.P.

After relating what had happened, the constable asked me if my son was receiving any type of treatment for his behaviour. I informed him of my son's diagnosis, and was able to provide him with the details of his medications, and his three weekly counsellors, all of which weighed in my son's favour.

We collected my son from the neighbour's yard, where he had been told to "Stay put!" by the constable. Then, the officer reprimanded the mother for not calling me and settling the matter between us, instead of calling the police to mediate it.

I felt somewhat better about my son's melt down, though had the mother simply returned his game, he wouldn't have acted out the way he did.

What had me baffled was the obvious fear that led her to barricade herself in her kitchen. If a neighbour's child was standing outside, shouting for his game to be returned and kicking my door, you can bet there would have been a different outcome.

I wasn't thrilled with my son's brush with the law, but it did serve me in good stead, for a time. Whenever he gave me major attitude, I reminded him about his experience. I wasn't above a pointed reminder...whatever worked.

Chapter 12

Facing Your Personal Demons

For years, I carried around the guilt that I was to blame for my son's behaviour. At times, I still feel guilty, but I have done my best to move past that and focus on helping my son.

Berating or chastising yourself for what you should have, would have, or could have done differently serves no purpose. What's done is done, and now you need to step up to the plate and work at effectively helping your child. To do that, you need to get past your feelings.

I didn't arrive at this conclusion overnight. I spent years feeling depressed and heartsick about my choices. I blamed myself, and accepted my son's behaviour as punishment for ruining his life.

> "Even before a child is born, certain parental or family characteristics increase the odds that the child will have ADHD...a child born into that family may be more likely to have ADHD than children born into families without those risk factors."
>
> Russell A. Barkley, PhD
> Taking Charge of ADHD

I cried a lot. When everyone was asleep, except my son and me, the guilt and frustration were overwhelming.

I never gave myself a break.

When friends would tell me what a wonderful mother I was. I would smile or laugh but inside I felt only guilt and shame.

I was tired all the time. Nothing I did seemed to make a difference. I actually did try personal counselling, or therapy, if you will, but all that came of it was a prescription for anti-depressants.

I tried the anti-depressants, but after a couple of days, I quit taking them because of the side effects. I would rather feel physically well and be depressed than feel nauseous but happy, so I decided not to take them.

I thought trying my hand at song writing might help channel some of my feelings. In order to be a good songwriter, you need to be depressed, don't you? After all, how many songs are there about losing someone, divorce, break-ups, accidents, broken hearts, and lost love?

It helped for a while and got my creativity flowing again, but aside from that, it created no significant change in my life.

I admit I was looking for a quick fix.

I was barely surviving on welfare, living well below the poverty line, had stress levels equivalent to an Air Traffic Controller, little respite except the odd hour I could occasionally beg, and there was no end in sight.

One of these days, I may stop colouring my hair just to see how many grey hairs I have. Lord knows, I've earned every one of them!

> "All of us get tired, stressed, angry, and short-sighted at times...It is the striving toward self-improvement that matters most, and all of us can succeed at committing ourselves to that course even though we fall short of it occasionally."
>
> Russell A. Barkley, PhD
> Taking Charge of ADHD

Placing blame is another trap we fall into. Blame is not something that can be placed squarely on one parent or the other, and makes no difference to your child, his counsellor, his teachers or his friends.

> "Your child was born with this problem; it is through no fault of his own...Likewise, you should neither assign blame to yourself nor accept it from others."
>
> Taking Charge of ADHD

Here is a news flash for you. Every parent who has a child with ADHD/ODD, ADD, Anxiety Disorder, Depression, Schizophrenia, and just about every other disorder or disability, is carrying around the same feeling that his or her actions might have been responsible to some extent.

They are correct in the belief that some part of who they are helped to shape their child's development. Current research is now pointing to some interesting statistics.

> "...heredity explains between 55% and 97% of the range of hyperactive and impulsive behaviour seen in children..."
>
> Taking Charge of ADHD

Science has determined that ADHD/ODD is more likely to be genetically inherited, in the same way as hair colour, height, and weight are passed on, than caused by environmental factors.

> "More recently, a number of studies have confirmed that at least two genes may be related to ADHD...D4RD, is related to the personality dimension known as *novelty seeking*...DAT1...has a particular form that is more commonly associated with ADHD than would be expected to occur...Besides these two genes, at least six others are now under investigation..."
>
> Taking Charge of ADHD

After I moved to Mission, I increased my efforts to help my son become successful in school. I was becoming familiar with the constant pressure of daily surprises regarding his behaviour.

I began celebrating the days where nothing happened. My son and I developed a routine, and I resigned myself to the reduced school attendance. I concentrated my efforts on helping the counsellors and teachers get a clearer picture of my son, and the guilt began to recede.

It didn't go away completely. I don't know if it ever will, but it was no longer crippling. After spending eight years wrestling with that demon, I was finally breaking free of its hold.

Now I could focus my attention on another one. This demon isn't self-generated, but the effect it has on my confidence is a force to be reckoned with.

I'm talking about society's perception of my child and my ability to parent him. Almost everyone has heard something about ADHD. Websites are springing up all over the World Wide Web, offering solutions, medication alternatives and support.

Yet even with all this information at our fingertips, the stigma of being a bad parent persists. I see it in the faces of people we meet. Whether out shopping, driving, waiting in line, in restaurants, or at a doctor's office, I can nearly always catch that glance of disapproval from at least one patron.

That glance speaks louder than words. It seems to scream, "Can't you control your child? What kind of parent are you, letting him run around like that?" Or, "If that was my kid I'd tan his hide."

I admit, before having my son, I was guilty of this outdated mindset too.

> "Understanding that ADHD is just an extreme form of a trait we all possess and that it is something people "come by naturally" should help everyone view ADHD from a kinder perspective."
>
> Taking Charge of ADHD

Once, I would have cringed and accepted the guilt and the blame. Now, though, I would love to see them take care of my son for two weeks. Then let's hear what they have to say about my parenting skills.

I'm still battling that demon. In its own way, this one is more insidious than guilt. Just when you think you have a handle on things, another person gives you that look, and the resentment rises up like floodwaters.

This mindset pervades our society. We value well-behaved children and have little tolerance for those who act out or are different, whatever the cause.

> "Science is showing us that there are neurological (brain) factors that contribute to self-control and willpower, along with learning and upbringing. And when these brain systems are functioning improperly or become damaged, normal levels of self-control and willpower are impossible."
>
> Taking Charge of ADHD

Having a child like my son though, could be seen as a blessing in disguise. I have more tolerance towards the social transgressions of other children, and more empathy with their parents.

> "...children without self-control are viewed either as not wanting to control themselves (they are "bad seeds") or as not having learned to control themselves (they are viewed as simply "undisciplined" by their parents)."
>
> Taking Charge of ADHD

I no longer see these children as only unruly, spoiled, undisciplined little tyrants bent on making everyone around them uncomfortable. Once you are familiar with the behaviours, you can easily spot them. Now, I watch them for signs of kinship with my own son.

Chapter 13

Winds of Change

Hmm, that sounds more like the title of a soap opera than a chapter heading, but it certainly reflects the sweeping alterations in the pattern of our lives. Even as my son and I were becoming more comfortable in our new place, my daughter was making noises of discomfort about her situation.

After much discussion, and some necessary rule setting, she had decided that she did want to live with us. This, of course, meant moving from our cozy little two-bedroom basement suite.

My daughter accepted she would have to sleep in the living room until we could find a suitable place. Fortunately, after my move from Surrey, I had acquired a new bed, and still had her futon, so she wasn't forced to camp out on a couch. Even so, it would be a bit of a tight squeeze for the three of us. I had the use of an attached garage, so we stored her furniture and whatever we couldn't fit in the house, and midway through my son's third year of school, she moved back home.

My son seemed pleased with the change. Even though he still balked at the idea that his sister could tell him what to do, he was proud that we were once again, a family.

He enjoyed walking home with his sister when she would pick him up after school. When she decided to learn how to drive, he happily took over the role of back seat driver.

Not everything was familial bliss however. My son still had his outbursts when things didn't go his way, but for the most part, my daughter was more empathetic towards him. She took responsibility for some of his home care, albeit somewhat grudgingly, and was much more supportive.

The counselling sessions appeared to be paying off, as his school attendance increased and the suspensions decreased. He still had a major issue with authority, rudeness and disrespect, but his threats of physical violence dwindled.

It was beginning to look like our move to Mission had been the right choice.

For the first time since my son started school, he was able to participate in sports day. Both my daughter and I showed up, not only for support, but in case our intervention was needed.

His attitude at times wavered a bit from the positive and he didn't participate in every event, but he managed the whole day with his class. I was immensely proud.

By the time he was promoted to Grade 4, he had progressed from going to school two hours in the morning, to full days – a huge step for my son.

Our new home, on the other hand turned out to be a disaster. The suite was quite nice, but the neighbours proved to be anything but. We spent the summer adjusting and trying to learn all the rules.

As the season progressed, we were regaled with snide comments, deliberately loud music first thing in the morning and late at night, loss of hot water and no water pressure while in the shower, as well as various petty confrontations.

My son couldn't get used to his new neighbourhood. The children next door weren't allowed out of their yard, and weren't allowed to play with him.

He wasn't allowed to play anywhere in our yard, because the other tenants were worried he might damage their property. The front yard was out of bounds, the side of the house was out of bounds, and he couldn't play in the back yard, which was technically ours to use, because he might break the shed where their things were stored.

The only place he could play without being yelled at was in the driveway at the back of the house.

I was soon informed that standing on the back porch and calling for my son was unacceptable. The other tenants didn't like it, and complained to our landlord. Now, I don't know about you, but when I grew up, all we heard at suppertime were parents calling their kids in to eat.

We had a large covered deck and my son would stand at the front of it and throw sticks over the edge. In his imagination, they were hand grenades and bombs, but to the person downstairs, they were another reason to yell at him – for not picking them up.

I would go out in the mornings and discover a pile of sticks or his broken toys lying in front of the door. Actually, anything that was discarded in the driveway or yard was put at my door, because, of course, it had to have been left by us.

We weren't to use the front driveway because the downstairs tenant claimed sole usage. Even the pizza delivery driver was yelled at for using it.

My daughter wasn't allowed to walk beside the house to get from the front to the back, because that disturbed the downstairs tenants.

She couldn't be dropped off or picked up in the front driveway, again because that was only for their use. We had the back access from the alley.

Such petty issues to cause such upset.

However, when the confrontations escalated, and my son was addressed crudely as a "(expletive deleted) psycho," and my daughter a "(expletive deleted) bitch," I decided it was time to go.

This wasn't the first time I had encountered problems with neighbours. It is very difficult to explain my son's behaviour and attitude in a way that others understand and accept.

I was used to scepticism from people, but this was the first time I had been faced with such total disbelief and antagonism. As far as this particular neighbour was concerned, my son didn't have any disabilities; he was just a delinquent – and I was a horrible parent.

The constant criticism, open hostility and shunning was not quite as bad as what we had faced in Surrey, but it came a very close second.

My son reacted by falling back into a destructive mindset, using sticks to whip the heads off flowers…and he started stealing.

That year, in Grade 4, he received more suspensions and citation slips for acting out than he had the first year we moved here. The only thing that kept him from complete regression was his counselling sessions.

He became more introverted. Always a bit of a loner, he now seemed to close the shutters and bar the door.

The one bright spot during that time was his first camping trip. He was somewhat anxious when we told him about the trip. He had never gone camping before, and had already made up his mind that he didn't like it.

My daughter and I decided for a first trip we would pick a civilized spot instead of roughing it, choosing a campground with an outdoor pool, playground, of course, a corner store, and paved roadways to all the camping spots.

He loved it! He played with the kids until after the sun set every night. He adored the pool, frog hunting, and feeding the ducks that wandered from one campsite to the next. Every morning, he was greeted by a gaggle of ducks clamouring for their morning crusts of bread.

While there were always signs of his ADHD, there were no episodes of ODD. He went to sleep easily and quickly, in part I believe, because we brought neither television nor video games. All in all, he was well behaved, and I was very proud of him on that trip.

Unfortunately, the good behaviour was not destined to last. Shortly after coming home from our camping trip, I received a phone call from a woman who used to live a couple of streets away from us.

She was phoning to inform me that my son had been vandalising her flowerbeds, and that her husband had arrived to find him and another boy digging holes and ripping up the flowers.

This was not good. It didn't matter that the house in question had been vacant for several months, except for a dog in the back yard. My son had taken to wandering into the backyard to visit the dog, and staying to play on the trampoline, as well as using the hose to water the lawn and gardens...and sometimes, the dog.

My son is irresistibly drawn to hoses and outside taps. When allowed, he will water lawns, gardens, fences and walls with complete abandon. Unfortunately, the owner of the house, who had been notified of this by a neighbour across the street, didn't appreciate my son's enthusiasm or his gardening skills, and the police were called.

I arrived before the police, to find the husband standing guard over the boys, while the wife surveyed the damage to the property. After apologising profusely, something I had become good at by this time, I told the boys to clean up their mess.

When the squad car arrived, the boys had nearly completed the job. The woman spoke with the constable, explaining the reason for the call, and showed him the damage.

The boys pleaded that they weren't trying to destroy her flowerbeds, explaining that as the house had been vacant for a long time, they were looking after it, weeding and watering the yard, and the dog.

Fortunately, for my son, the officer did not haul him away in handcuffs. He did however, give him a very stringent warning about getting into trouble, and explained what would happen if they were called out again. To this day, my son has not forgotten that warning.

Things had changed at my son's school as well. The principal he had grown very fond of over the past year and a half was transferred to another school part way through my son's Grade 4 year.

His replacement, although capable in his job, did not hold the same tolerance for my son's outbursts in school, and the out-of-school suspensions started up again.

I did my best to explain to him that sending my son home was not the solution, but he would not budge from his viewpoint.

He conceded that the school was caught "between a rock and a hard place" with regards to my son's unwillingness to conform and do his class work, but that unfortunately, "the school just could not tolerate his on-going defiance".

I had hoped the problems with my son's schooling were behind me. I had found a school run by caring professionals who were willing to work with my son, who accepted that I had useful information and insights, and listened when I offered comments and suggestions. Now all that changed.

Once again, the battle lines had been drawn, and I found myself facing a wall of bureaucracy, with the teachers, principal and school board regulations on one side, and me and my son on the other.

Chapter 14

Insight

When we moved to our third new neighbour-hood, in as many years, the change in my son was like night and day, at least for the first week. He listened when I asked him to do something, he answered me when I called him, he was polite, he played well with the neighbour children, and there were no outbursts of bad behaviour.

I thought someone had swapped kids when I wasn't looking. This couldn't be my son!

I didn't have long to wait before the ODD reared its ugly head and showed me the honeymoon was over, but for that short, wonderful time, I caught another glimpse of the loving boy who lay behind the disability.

I know my son can be a caring individual. I see it when he stops to pet a cat, or talks to a stranger about their dog. He loves bunnies, and cute fuzzy stuffed animals. I see it when he comes up to me wanting a hug, just because.

Unfortunately, the disabilities prevent that loving boy from being present all the time. Not only is it hard for his teachers, friends, family, and society in general to understand him, it is equally hard for him.

He doesn't understand why he says and does, as he puts it, "bad things." He struggles with the concept that people don't like him, and that he has trouble making friends. He is unable to grasp the complexities of social interaction that we take for granted.

Nearly every community, in every country, has children and families like mine struggling to find their way, just like me. Studies have shown that 5 – 8% of all children in the United States have ADHD. This translates to over two million kids under the age of eighteen, and doesn't include Canada, or the rest of the world.

The U.S. is the world leader in the quantity of research and volume of publications on mental health disorders in children. However, other countries such as Canada, England,

Australia, and Holland have shown an increase in professional knowledge about ADHD, and the rates of diagnoses and prescription medications now available to treat this disorder have risen proportionately.

Findings of the last fifteen years reveal that ADHD/ODD exists in every country and ethnic group that has been studied to date.

> "New Zealand, 2-7%; Germany, 4%; India, 5-29%; China, 6-9%; Japan, 7-8%; the Netherlands, 1-3%; of teenagers, (children not studied); and Brazil, 5-6%."
> " ...it is safe to conclude, then, that ADHD is a universal disorder that is found in all countries."
>
> Russell A. Barkley, PhD
> Taking Charge of ADHD

This would mean that approximately fourteen million kids worldwide have ADHD.

Studies have shown that if an early pattern of ADHD/ODD lasts for a year or longer, it will probably continue into childhood and teenage years, and that 50 – 65% of children with ADHD will continue to have symptoms as an adult.

Most of them will have jobs and be self-sufficient, however their educational levels and economic status is likely to be lower. As well, at least 20 – 45% will have trouble with anti-social behaviours.

Gone are the days when "children should be seen and not heard." The phrase, "When I was your age," no longer applies when it comes to raising our kids. Nowadays, in order to be a good parent, we almost need a degree in psychology just to understand the workings of our social structure.

With all the technical advances like cell phones, i-pods, home computers and instant downloads, we have had to change the way we prepare our children for their future.

Most of us easily embrace these changes, but what works for the majority, doesn't for many of these families. Parents of ADHD/ODD children can feel they are swimming against the current, like so many wrong-headed fish.

Society needs to be made aware of the challenges these kids face, *on a daily basis.*

Look at the school system, for example. They supply teacher's aides, and in some cases, Child Care Workers, but these workers often don't have the knowledge or training to cope with these children.

The behavioural program that was so highly touted at the school my son attended for Grade 2 is an example of that.

The workers were grasping at straws when it came to my son. They looked for outside influences as the reasons for his disruptive behaviour. They couldn't comprehend why integration into a normal classroom setting was not working.

They did not understand that the behaviours were not the effect of external issues – they were caused by the disability, the inability to filter thought and action.

I can't help feeling disillusioned and frustrated – disillusioned by the system, by the lack of information readily available before diagnosis, and frustrated by having to ferret out almost every scrap of information and valuable contact on my own.

Life would be so much easier if the professionals were all operating from the same system. Then, we would be far less likely to overlook a sometimes-necessary step in helping our children.

I have discovered since travelling this road that until our children exhibit serious, socially disturbing behaviour, most often in a school setting, we are left to do the best we can.

I would have appreciated help with my son's sleep patterns. As he was so young, it wasn't apparent he had a disability, but there must be studies of other babies with severe sleep irregularities.

Yet the only solutions offered were the methods I was already using. No information or support groups were mentioned, and testing wasn't considered.

I remember the relief I experienced when I was told about Melatonin. After years of frustration, just by chance, I was told about a little pill, a natural sleep aid. Had I know of it sooner, it could have made a world of difference.

> "In encounters with physicians and mental health specialists, parents of a child with ADHD have been dismissed as hysterical, easily stressed, or naive, especially if the child was well behaved during the appointment."
>
> Taking Charge of ADHD

I don't know if one exists yet, but we need some kind of Appendix, or Glossary, or "See Also" listing, that details additional problems these children might also experience, such as learning disabilities.

Barring that, at least a "What Should Be Done Next" list could be supplied so that parents can be pointed towards the necessary resources instead of having to seek them out blindly, stumble across them by accident, or search them out one by one at the local library, or on the internet.

It's very hard to locate a treasure when you can't find the map.

The problem with raising a child with this disability is that we feel as if we are lost on a desert island. We can spend years searching for clues and solutions before we discover other parents who are struggling with the same things we are. Not surprisingly, these are the very people who pass on bits of advice and resources.

Support groups for families living with this disability are of critical importance, however, they need more than just support. Even if you discover your child doesn't have ADHD, it would be invaluable to have a source of information that might help you deal with the challenges you are facing.

It's unfortunate that many professionals seem uninterested in our plight. As long as these children are viewed as "unruly delinquents," "psycho children," or worse, as long as the fear and discrimination continues unchecked, these children and their families will continue to be shunned and marginalized.

That this hasn't received the same level of media attention as so many other disabilities suggests how marginalized the families of ADHD children have become.

I know I'm not the only parent out there having these problems. Hundreds of parents and caregivers face these same challenges. One voice may not be enough to bring about major changes within the system, but one voice can grow into many, and we need to be heard.

> "Many parents of children with ADHD have told me of the shame and humiliation they have experienced at the hands of educators and professionals...Some have described feeling lost or misunderstood or being treated like children themselves...They felt that their views and opinions were dismissed as biased or naive. Their overall impression was that those involved simply wanted to reach some quick conclusion – to do what was cheap and expedient...not what was best for the child."
>
> Taking Charge of ADHD

Hopefully, my story will help to bring this undeclared epidemic into the light. We need to educate others on what it's like trying to rear a child with behavioural issues, and help bring about some much needed changes for parents like us.

We need to educate our teachers and healthcare workers. We need programs specifically for ADHD/ODD children and their families in our communities, because without them, we will have failed to give these kids the help and resources necessary to ensure their place in society.

I am passionate about my son's well-being. I have seen the wonderful, loving, funny, normal child behind the disability, and I know there are other parents out there who feel the same way I do.

> "You are the *case manager* of your child's life, and you must be a proactive executive prepared to take charge – and to keep it longer than most parents must...You are the child's advocate with others in the community who control the resources you will need."
>
> Taking Charge of ADHD

Epilogue

Currently, my son is in Grade 6. After receiving notice of my son's third suspension within the span of a week, I have learned he will be repeating his year.

> "Anywhere from 23% to 35% of children with ADHD will be retained in a grade at least once before reaching high school, mostly in the early elementary years."
>
> Russell A. Barkley, PhD
> Taking Charge of ADHD

As well, I have made contact with the Learning Disability Association of Canada.

I have learned that many children with ADHD have an underlying learning disability that prevents them from being successful in the classroom. This was new information for me, and had not been addressed before by any of the many professionals I had consulted thus far.

Although I had been asked if my son had any learning disabilities, and always replied,

"None that I know of…" no one ever suggested it might be useful to have him tested to be sure his behaviours weren't fuelled at least in part by an underlying learning disability.

I should have seen this coming. Having dealt with this lack of information, interest, and concern since the birth of my son, I should no longer be surprised by it.

The Learning Disabilities spokesperson was even less surprised than I was. I was told the Association butted heads with school districts regularly, and was familiar with the cavalier attitude displayed by many professionals when deciding what information to pass on to the parents.

Here, though, I was graciously allowed to browse the Association's extensive library, given resource materials, pamphlets, a list of steps to take, and told they would be happy to provide any other help they could. From famine to feast!

I highly recommend a visit to their website, and I have provided the information at the end of the chapter, along with a list of suggested reading materials. I hope you find them useful.

If you are fortunate enough to have a child like mine, know that you are not alone. I salute your dedication and offer a quotation from a fellow Canadian who wisely said, "...Keep your stick on the ice..."

Sources:

- Barkley, Russell A. PhD, *Taking Charge of ADHD – The complete authoritative guide for parents*. Guilford Press, New York, revised 2005

- Barkley, Russell A. & C. M. Benton, *Your Defiant Child: Eight steps to better behaviour*. Guilford Press, New York, 1998

- Caroll, Lee & Jan Tober, *The Indigo Children*. Hay House, Carlsbad, CA, 1999

Suggested Reading:

- Bain, L. *A, Parent's Guide to Attention Deficit Disorders*. Delta/Dell, New York, 1991

- Cohen, M.W., *The Attention Zone: A Parent's guide to Attention Deficit/Hyperactivity Disorder*. Brunner/Mazel, Philadelphia, 1998

- Fowler, M. C., *CHADD educators' manual*. CASET Associates, Plantation, Fl, 1992

Additional Resources:

- Learning Disabilities Association of Canada – www.ldac-acta.ca

- Learning Disabilities Association of America – www.ldanatl.org

- CHADD National Headquarters – (800) 233-4050 www.chadd.org

- ADDA – (847) 432-ADDA www.add.org

- Thanet ADDers Kent, England – (0) 1843 851145 www.adders.org   email: simon@adders.org

- www.livingwithadhdodd.blogspot.com

- www.alt.support.attn-deficit

- www.btinternet.com/~black.ice/addnet/

- www.pavilion.co.uk/add/

Printed in Great Britain
by Amazon.co.uk, Ltd.,
Marston Gate.